THE OFFICIAL
REDNECK HANDBOOK

D0954174

THE OFFICIAL
REDNECK HANDBOOK

BO WHALEY

Rutledge Hill Press
NASHVILLE, TENNESSEE 37210

Copyright © 1987 Bo Whaley

All rights reserved. Written permission must be secured from the publisher to use or reproduce any part of this book, except for brief quotations in critical reviews or articles.

Published in Nashville, Tennessee, by Rutledge Hill Press, Inc., 513 Third Avenue South, Nashville, Tennessee 37210

Recipes on pages 46, 47, and 48 are taken from *Kiss My Grits!* copyright © 1984 by Roy Overcast and used with permission. Copies of *Kiss My Grits!* may be obtained from Roy Overcast Associates, 2301 12th Avenue South, Nashville, Tennessee 37204.

Library of Congress Cataloging-in-Publication Data

Whaley, Bo, 1926-
  The official redneck handbook.

    1. Southern States—Social life and customs—
Anecdotes, facetiae, satire, etc. 2. Working
class whites—Southern States—Anecdotes, facetiae,
satire, etc. I. Title.
PN6231.S64W43 1987   305.5'62   87-12708
ISBN 0-934395-48-9

        13 14 15 16 17 18 19—95 94 93 92
Manufactured in the United States of America

WHAT, EXACTLY, IS A REDNECK? This is a question that has cried out for an answer ever since Adam popped the first wad of Levi Garrett in his mouth and Eve cautioned him not to spit on the Astroturf.

Here, then, are the conclusions of one redneck researcher who has considered the question for more than forty years.

A redneck is a mysterious sort of character who drives a four-wheel drive pickup with oversize tires on the first floor and a cab perched on the eighth, flanked by twin CB antennas, with a fish stringer hanging from the inside rear-view mirror. He's a shaggy-haired varmint who hasn't seen a barber since Sal Maglie retired from baseball, sports a beard, and wears a Cat Diesel cap, black with yellow patch. In his left shirt pocket is a barely visible pouch of Levi Garrett chewing tobacco, with an equally subdued pack of Winstons in his right. A 30.06 rifle (with scope) and a .12 gauge Remington Model 1100 shotgun, along with a reel and rod, hang in the back window above the decal of a Confederate flag that bears the reminder: "Hell No! I Ain't Forgettin'!" And there are three bumper stickers: "How 'Bout Them Dawgs?!," "Get Your Heart in America or Get Your (picture of a donkey) Out!," and next to it is one with a forefinger pointed skyward that says "I Found It!"

Those are the back bumper. On the front under the grille is a personalized tag that reads, "Joe Boy and Willie Kate."

He's driving with a long-neck Bud in one hand, a large portion of Willie Kate in the other, and they listen as Waylon and Willie and the boys knock out their theme song, "Luckenbach, Texas," on the AM-FM stereo tape player.

And, they're headed to . . . wherever, to do . . . whatever.

To **Robbie Nell Bell.**
To know her
is to love her.
I know her,
and I love her.

CONTENTS

INTRODUCTION

A recent Yankee visitor to Dixieland was overheard inquiring of a born and bred redneck, "Tell me, just what do you find to do here in this part of the country?"

"Well, one thing we do is spend a lot of time givin' thanks to the Good Lord," the redneck replied.

"Giving thanks? For what?"

"For the privilege of bein' 'lowed to live here."

The migration of Yankees to the South is at an all-time high these days. This should not surprise us when we pause to consider the prophetic words of that great son of the South, Col. Beauregard P. Hornsby, who said, "I say, son . . . now you ain't never heard of nobody retirin' to th' Nawth, have you?"

This book will prove invaluable to the thundering herds moving to the South daily. It will help them understand their new home. It will also be useful to born rednecks in keeping up their self-image and serve as a guide to prevent their falling prey to the Yankee way of doin' things. The book will have served a valuable purpose if it protects just one good ol' boy from bein' corrupted.

The sons and daughters of the South have long been regarded as compassionate and forgiving souls. We will do everything in our power to try to ensure that those fortunate Yankees relocating South find the transition as smooth and painless as possible. However, there is one request: Don't tell us "how you done it in New Jersey," because to be perfectly honest with you, we really don't give a damn how you done it in New Jersey . . . or New York . . . or Boston.

As I strolled along the boulevard in Jacksonville Beach, I spotted a sign on the front door of Jack's Submarine Shop. When I read it, I knew Jack was my kind of man:

"There will be a $5 service charge to listen to how beautiful, how big, and how cheap everything is up north."
—Thank you, The Management

The management? That would be Jack Salter, owner and sole employee of Jack's Sub Sandwich Shop.

I walked inside and found a man with a white beard seated at a table partaking of a can of beer and a ham and cheese sandwich and reading the newspaper.

"Mornin'," I said.

"Yep, sure is," he said. "Right on up to twelve o'clock. Happens ever' day."

I couldn't argue with that.

"What'll you have?" he asked.

"Well, actually, I just came in because I like your sign on the front door," I replied. "Already had breakfast. Just loafing."

"Fine. Sit down an' have a cup o' coffee, or a beer," he said.

"Well, coffee sounds good. I'll have a cup o' coffee with you."

I was well into the coffee when I mentioned the sign again. He responded quickly:

"Put that sign up three years ago," Jack said. "I been down here for fourteen years. Retired from General Motors in Flint, Michigan. Nobody but me, so I opened this little sandwich shop. I finally got tired of all the Yankees runnin' down the South so I put up the sign. And you know we've got oodles of Yankees down here. You couldn't run 'em back up north with a machine gun."

"Aren't they offended by the sign?" I asked.

"Offended?" he asked. "Hell, you can't offend a Yankee! They've got it made down here, and they know it."

"But, and no offense intended, Jack, aren't you a Yankee?" I asked.

"Was," he said. "But that ended June 1, 1970, the day I

loaded up my ol' Buick an' headed south. When I crossed the Mason-Dixon Line I was converted."

We live in an open society here in America and every-body has a right to be a redneck. *The Official Redneck Handbook* will help everyone know what one is. Rednecks don't wear tattoos or wrist bands identifying themselves as such. Therefore it is very difficult for urban southerners to recognize them and virtually impossible for Yankees to make the transformation south without first having at least some knowledge regarding the breed.

Some people are born rednecks ("they have natural tal-ent"), but others have to work hard at it. This book is for both kinds. For those forced to work at it, *The Official Redneck Handbook* is a "how to" book. Once the knack of being a redneck has been mastered, those unfortunate souls remaining "above the line" shoveling snow and fighting traf-fic will envy their counterparts no end.

Many an aspiring youngster has said, "When I grow up, I want to be a redneck." This book will provide invaluable assistance in helping them get there, and without making any wrong turns. They deserve no less.

So *The Official Redneck Handbook* serves two purposes: to assist Yankees bent on retiring South so that they will be better prepared to accept and cope with life below the Mason-Dixon Line—which is actually nothing more than the dividing line between "You'se guys" and "Y'all"—and to point out to those of us who already live here the many blessings we enjoy.

After having read this handbook, anybody will be able to cope anywhere in the South, no matter where he was born and raised. He will know how to talk, what to eat, where to go (and where not to go), how to dress, what social functions to attend, how to hunt and fish, how to cook what he catches and kills, what juke joints the real Rednecks come to roost in, how to furnish and decorate a doublewide, and just what makes a Redneck tick. Also, he will be able to under-stand conversations without benefit of an interpreter.

And this book is a must for "closet rednecks." They should never leave home without it.

So, let's get on with it. Let's get down to the nitty gritty. We have mountains of material to cover. As the saying goes way down in grits country, "Let's let it all hang out!"

SECTION ONE

RELOCATIONS REQUIRES PREPARATION

HOW CAN YANKEES BLEND IN WITH SOUTHERN LIVING?

This is an open letter to those thundering herds of carpetbaggers who are seriously considering migrating south into Georgia, Texas and other Southern states.

It ain't easy to just pull up stakes and move off to a new region of the country and blend in immediately. Just ask any good ol' Southern boy forced to move north to Chicago, Detroit, Newark or New York City.

But if you are bound and determined to make the move to Dixie, here are some tips on how a Yankee can ease into the redneck life in the South with minimal difficulty. (Note: These tips apply to all states south of the Mason-Dixon line except Florida, which is really nothing more than one giant rest home for New York City and New Jersey folks.)

O.K., here we go.

• Sell your BMW. It screams "Yankee" at every turn.

• Buy a pickup truck, preferably 1973–78 vintage.

• Add a gun rack across the rear window of the cab and replace the conventional tires with big 'uns.

• Install a tape player and buy two tapes to start with, "Moe and Joe Bandy" and "Waylon and Willie and the Boys."

• Weld a trailer hitch to the back bumper and place a hound dog of dubious lineage in the back. Name him "Scrap Iron."

• Go to the nearest five and ten, buy a pair of those big fuzzy dice and hang them from the rear view mirror. If you have a pair of baby shoes and the tassel from your graduation cap, hang them, too.

These things accomplished, you will have taken a giant step in the direction toward gaining provisional status as a good ol' boy in the South. But disregard the above if it is your intention to re-locate in Atlanta. It ain't a Southern city no more, what with the Yankee money taking over and all. Shoot! In Atlanta now a fellow has to go days on end without hearing a Southern accent, and English itself is struggling to remain afloat.

Be that as it may, here's a word about dress for those staying on Interstate 75 and ignoring Atlanta for points further South:

• Learn to dress casually. Divest yourself of those tight-fitting designer suits and lizard-skin Italian shoes that seem to be so popular with certain New Yorkers and short, swarthy, just-arrived South American Latins.

• Ideally, you should have two wardrobes of jeans. The dirt-slicked, worn-out-at-the-knees kind (with a circular imprint of a snuff can on the rear pocket) will suffice for everyday wear. But you'll need a couple of faded, but clean pairs with razor-sharp creases down the front for Sundays and special occasions. You know, like the ones them Grand Ole Opry stars wear with their tuxedo coats at the Country Music Awards show on television. But no belt. Don't wear no belt. That ain't macho.

• And whatever you do, don't be seen in public in a pair of designer jeans. Good ol' boys just flat don't wear Calvin Kleins in Dixie—dead or alive. But if you've got some, don't throw 'em away. Save 'em for when you go back to New York on vacation.

• Forget the blue oxford cloth button-down preppy dress shirts like you and your old lady wear. T-shirts with gross sayings on them will serve the purpose just fine. Be sure and get at least one with *Harley Davidson* on it.

• For special occasions and Sundays, a denim work shirt and leather jacket that looks like it was made from your grandmother's old oilcloth tablecloth is as near as a good ole boy comes to haute couture.

• Depending on your job, you may have to do something with your hair. Office workers, lawyers and assorted other professionals can get by with hair carefully groomed and frozen into place with hair spray. But . . . if your plan is to work in construction, road building, sheetrock hanging, becoming a country music singer or hitting the unemployment line upon arrival, you dang well better let it grow long.

• Pick up a cheap, used guitar and learn a couple of songs before you head south. Country songs are strongly suggested, something like "Release Me," and maybe "Born to Lose."

• Forget that skeet shooting and archery ever existed. These Yankee luxuries are practiced in the deep south only on South Carolina and south Georgia plantations owned by the ultimate carpetbaggers—David Rockefeller, William F. Buckley and John Hay Whitney. Forget them and find yourself a local coon hunting club. If there's not one around the area where you locate, there's always the weekly Lion's Club turkey shoot.

• Right off, start hanging around the neighborhood Amoco station in the evening and the pool room in the daytime. It's good practice for standing around outside a church on Wednesday night talkin' huntin' and fishin' with the other boys while the wife and the young 'uns are inside at prayer meeting.

• Learn to spit a lot. Rednecks and good ole boys are big spitters.

• Pay your child support on time.

• Understand there are some things you will be expected to get excited about: Fishing, hunting, motorcycles, pickup trucks, dogs, 18-wheelers, the Grand Ole Opry, Levi Garrett chewing tobacco, wrestling, gospel music, and county fairs.

• Learn to talk with a kitchen match in your mouth.

• Leave your list of vintage wines in Yankeeland. Beer's the name of the game in Dixie.

Finally, your name.

• If your name happens to be Maurice or Bruce, you'll never make it in redneck country unless you make the switch to initials. Start now calling yourself "M.C." or "J.D."

• Of course, you could go all the way and have you name legally changed to Bubba, the ultimate redneck status symbol. It will open almost as many doors for you as, well, Robert E. Lee.

• Females can't go wrong by assuming double names. Ethel, Penelope, Gertrude or Sheila won't get it. Such names as Robbie Nell, Willie

Kate, Martha Ann, Johnnie Faye, Gloria Jean, Kathy Sue and Mattie Bee guarantee almost immediate acceptance without explanation.

If you can bring yourself to make these suggested adjustments you are well on your way to making the move to redneck country.

But, there is more.

THE OFFICIAL REDNECK APTITUDE TEST

Self-appointed experts from the deep South and the far North keep trying to identify and classify the redneck. Some of them know what they're talking about, and some don't.

To aid them in their efforts I have designed what I believe is a foolproof aptitude test for the purpose of determining an individual's redneck traits or tendencies. You would do well to take the test. Better still, take it with a friend who is convinced he's a bigger redneck than you are. Make a friendly wager. Let the loser pay for the long-neck Buds.

REDNECK APTITUDE TEST

	Me	You
1. You get five points if you chew tobacco. Add two more if you dip snuff. You get an additional fifteen points if your grandmother dips snuff. Double that if you've ever kissed a woman who had snuff in her mouth at the time.	___ ___ ___	___ ___ ___
2. You get five points if you go swimming in cut-off Levis. If you are female and you wear cut-off Levis and a T-shirt swimming, you get double points. Both male and female subtract ten points if you do your swimming in a swimming pool. But add five points if your dog goes in swimming with you.	___ ___ ___	___ ___ ___

3. If you own a polyester leisure suit, give yourself five points. Add five more if you still wear it. Add three more points if you got it from your daddy. Double that if it has any embroidery on it.

———   ———

4. Give yourself three points if your belt has your name on the back. Add one point for each inch wide the buckle is. Add five points if you carry a knife in a case on the belt. You get five bonus points if you wear a white belt. If you wear white shoes to match the belt, add ten points. And if you wear white socks, add fifteen points.

———   ———

5. Give yourself five points if you wear cowboy boots. Double it if you sleep in them. Triple it if the boots are made of snake or lizard skin. Subtract fifteen points if they're made in Taiwan or in Massachussetts. Add ten points if you own a horse.

———   ———

6. You get ten points if you live in a mobile home. Add five more if it's a single-wide. Add two more for every dog that sleeps under it and one point for every tire that's rotted out. Add three for every sliding closet door that works but subtract three points if it's skirted, unless the skirting is rusted tin roofing or cardboard. Add one point for every dish in the sink that needs washing, but subtract a point for every pair of clean socks in the trailer.

———   ———

7. Give yourself ten points for every car in the yard that's up on cement blocks. Subtract two points for each cement block that you bought. Add one point for each year if it's older than a 1972 model. Subtract five points if it has a battery. Subtract ten points if it's a European sports car. Add ten if you painted it yourself with a brush. Add five if you had it painted by Earl Shieb.

8. Score ten points for yourself if you can whistle through your teeth. Add five more if your wife can.

9. Give yourself two points for every rifle you own, and add one point for each one with a scope. And give yourself five points if you carry a pistol in the glove compartment of your vehicle. Double that if your wife carries one, too. Triple it if she knows how to use it. Subtract ten points if either of you have a permit.

10. You get five points if you drive a pickup truck. Add five more if it's a four-wheel drive. Add five more if it has over-sized tires with raised white letters. Add another five if there's a dog box in the back, but subtract ten if the dog is registered. Add one point for every beer can in the back, add one point for each can that is hand-crushed. Subtract three points if the cooler is clean.

11. Give yourself four points if you smoke non-menthol cigarettes; and add five more if you smoke non-filter Camels. Subtract five if you don't smoke cigarettes. Add five points if you use stick matches, and two more if you can strike them with your thumbnail or on the seat of your britches. Add another for every hour you keep one in your mouth.

12. Give yourself five points if you've got a boat parked in the yard. Add three if it's a bass boat but subtract three if there are no dead worms in the bottom. Subtract five points if the motor cranks on the first pull. Subtract fifteen if it's a sailboat.

13. Give yourself five points if you have a beard, but subtract three if you bathed yesterday. Add three if all the plumbing works and all your utilities are paid and current.

14. You get five points if you wear a white shirt with the sleeves rolled up. Add five more if the shirttail is out. Subtract one point if it only has one pocket but add a point for each missing button. You must subtract two points if the collar button has ever been buttoned.

15. You get five points if you dropped out of high school. Double that if you were kicked out for fighting. Triple it if you attended for twelve years but failed to graduate.

16. Give yourself twenty points if you listen to country music. Add ten more if you've ever been to Nashville, and ten more if you went to the Grand Ole Opry. Subtract ten if you attended but didn't yell. You lose five more if you don't know where Johnny Cash and Merle Haggard served time. But add five if you can find WSM on your radio.

17. You lose ten points if you know who Pat Benetar is. And you lose twenty if you've ever listened to a whole song by Pat Benetar without changing to another station. You're out of the game and lose by forfeit if you own a Pat Benetar album or tape. But you can be considered for a future game if you can name all four members of the Alabama band.

Total   ———   ———

W ell, how did you make out? If you feel that you scored high enough to seriously consider making the move South, then you need to keep reading for some helpful hints before making a final decision.

SPEAKIN' REDNECK MADE EASY

Don't think for a minute that you can just up and move to redneck country and know what's goin' on right from the very start. Not so. Therefore, it is strongly suggested that you burn the ol' midnight oil in an attempt to memorize as many redneck words and phrases as possible before making the move. Otherwise, you will be just as lost as a redneck in China. You probably wouldn't understand a thing that's said.

There are certain key words that you'll need to know, words that come as natural as rain to a redneck. Having these words at your disposal will greatly ease the transformation.

The words selected have the same meaning north of the Mason-Dixon Line as they do south of it; the only real difference lies in their pronunciation.

By the way, no attempt is being made here to list the words in alphabetical order because it really don't make no difference as I see it. After all, we don't talk in alphabetical order, right?

The redneck spelling of the word is followed by the correct spelling of the word in parentheses. I figure you'll know that, but I ain't takin' no chances. Then there will be an example of how the word can be used in a sentence.

It is also suggested that this section of the book be clipped and saved because you never know when it might come in handy in your new surroundings.

NEVER LEAVE HOME WITHOUT IT!

Word	How It's Used
Kreck *(Correct):*	The kreck spellin' of kreck is "Correct." Lak "My mommer is a skool teecher and tonite she has to kreck tes' papuhs."
Fem *(Film):*	"My an' Buster went to th' maountins an' I tuk my camra, but I'll be dadgummed if'n I did'n f'rgit to buy some fem."
Doc *(Dark):*	"I'm 19 yeers ol' but I steel sleep with a lite on 'cause I'm skeert o' th' doc."
Idnit *(Isn't it):*	"It shore is purty out t'nite with th' full moon an' all, idnit?"
Hard *(Hired):*	"My Daddy went to th' unemployment offis this mornin' to see 'bout gittin' a job at the new factry whut's openin' nex' month, but for some reason he wan't hard."
Idy *(Idea):*	"I heered whut ya' sed at th' PTA meetin' las' nite 'bout sponsorin' a chittlin' suppah to raise money f'r th' ban uniforms, Charlotte, an' I thank thas a reel gud idy."
Jevver *(Did you ever):*	"Bobby Joe tol' me ya' wuz daown at th' Chivverlay place lookin' at one o' them new Impallers. Jevver trade?"
Keer *(Care):*	"Granny ain't gittin' 'long so good, what with her a' havin' roomytisem an' all. But she's a' doin' bettah since she got on a program called Home Hailth Keer whur nurses come t' visit her to home onc't a week."
Mere *(Mirror):*	"We bin doin' th' crazies' thangs lately in Play Skool, Mary Frances. That

new teecher has got us mem'rizin silly verses. Yistitty we had t' larn one whut goes, "Mere, mere, on th' wahl, who's th' faires' uv them awl. Now then, I ast ya, ain't thet plum' silly?"

Wail *(Well):*
"I jis come fum th' doctor. I ain't rilly bin wail fer a while but wuz too busy to go an' find out whut wuz wrong. Found out I got shootin' pains, whatever th' heck that is."

Argy *(Argue):*
"I ain't a' goin' to Lucy Mae's no more. She thanks she knows ever'-thang an' she don't know nuthin' a tall. 'Sides, ever time I go to her haouse, all we ivver do is argy."

Bub *(Bulb):*
"Johnnie Faye! Run daoun to Mr. Johnson's stow an' git me a lite bub—hunnert watt."

Earl *(Aerial):*
"Josh, we plum' got to buy us a new earl fer th' radio. It's done got to th' pint whur I can't even git WSM an' they ain't no way I ain't gonna' lissen to th' Gran' Ole Opry come Sat'dy nite."

Far *(Fire):*
"Bobby Joe, go git some stovewood an' bild a far in th' farplace in th' livin' room. Granny's a' comin' this afternoon an' you know how she hates col' weather."

Cocoler *(Coca-Cola):*
"I want two hamburgers all the way, a awder o' Franch fries an' a Cocoler."

Hep *(Help):*
"Tell ya' whut I'll do, Lunce. If'n you'll hep me dig my 'taters, I'll hep you cut yore hay."

Awduh *(Order):*
"I'm gonna' awduh me two dresses an' a hat fum Sears. An' I'm gonna' awduh two pair of ovalls fer Jayssie."

Wudnit *(Wasn't it)*: "Boy! Thet shore wuz some scary movie on th' TV las' nite, wudnit?"

All *(Oil)*: "Lemme hav five dollars wuth o' reg'lar an' a quat o' all, Goober. Ever'thin' ailse is awright."

Bard *(Borrowed)*: "Lucy, I ain't loanin' Buster Bland nothin' ailse. He bard my shovel an' didn't brang hit bak. An' he bard my battry charger an' lost hit."

Bleeve *(Believe)*: "Wail, I kin tail ya' one thang 'baout ol' man Jenkins. Ya' jus' can't bleeve a word he says. I wouldn't bleeve 'im if he wuz a' dyin' an' knowed it."

Kumpny *(Company)*: "Git in heah an' blow yo nose an' warsh yore face, young'un! Don't ya' know we got kumpny a' comin t'nite?"

Gull *(Girl)*: "Who wuz zat gull I seen ya' with las' nite, Bobby Jack? Man! She wuz a hum-dinger!"

Orta *(Ought to)*: "I know dang wail I orta go ahead an' git my new car tag, but I jus' can't never thank uv it when I'm in taoun."

Nome *(No m'am)*: "Robert! Is ya' did yor Ainglish homework yit?" "Nome." "Wail, git on hit this minit! Fus' thang ya' know you'll be growed up an' won't have no idy haow t' write 'er tawk a tall."

Rench *(Rinse)*: "I used to hav' a bunch o' troubl' with bad breath, m'sef. But I bought me some o' that stuff I seen on the TV whut ya' rench aout ya' mouth with an' I ain't had no more troubl'."

Tarred *(Tired)*: "Why 'ont y'all go on to th' pitcher show, Zeke. I bin arnin' awl day an' I'm tarred aout."

Yale *(Yell):*

"Wail naow, Bessie Faye, ya' can't be no cheerleader if'n ya' ain't willin' t' yale. Shoot! You can yale with the bes' uv 'em, so git on aout there an' yale."

Umurkin *(American):*

"Did'ja see that feller on th' lebbum o' clock news las' nite burnin' that Umurkin flag up in New Yawk? Sumbody orta' raound him up an' teech 'im a lesson with a tar arn or sum'thin. I don't bleeve he's no Umurkin, nohow."

Treckly *(Later):*

"Y'all go on home an' feed the cows an' slop th' hawgs, Lena. I'll be comin' on treckly."

Whirr *(Where):*

"Whirr you bin, boy? Suppah's bin redy f'r mor'n two ouers."

Ovalls *(Overalls):*

"Somebody answer that tellyphone, an' tell whoever 'tis I'll be there soon's I hang these ovalls on th' line."

Smore *(Some more):*

"Ma, kin I hav smore greeuts?"

Spear *(Superior):*

"Daddy said Buddy got coat-marshulled 'cuz he cuassed his spear oficer."

Rernt *(Ruined)*: "Know that new coat I bought at th' sale las' week? Well, Harvey spil't battry acid on it an' rernt it."

Prolly *(Probably)*: "I ain't reel shore whut we gonna' do this Crismus. We'll prolly go to Mama's."

Summers *(Somewhere)*: "I 'ont know zackly whirr Chicargo's at, but I believe hit's summers up north close to Illernoise."

Arn *(Iron)*: "I tell ya', Hoss, thet ol' boy's tough as pig arn."

Aig *(Egg)*: "Yeah, I bin t' Savanner twice't. An both times I went thet papuh meal smelt lak a rotten aig."

Plike *(Play like)*: "Tell ya' whut, Billy Frank; you plike you Tonto and I'll plike I'm th' Lone Ranger."

Ahmoan *(I'm going to)*: "Ahmoan ast Ma if I kin spen' th' nite at yore house."

Fur *(Far)*: "How fur it is fum Atlanter to Chattnooger?"

Munt *(Month)*: "Febererry is th' shortes' munt uf th' yeer."

Moanin *(Morning)*: "Good moanin', Mr. Weeulson."

Hail *(Hell)*: "Wail, I'll jus' tail ya' haow I feel 'bout it. If'n she don't lak th' way I dress, she can jus' go straight to hail."

Airs *(Errors)*: "Anybody whut plays baseball is baound to make airs 'cause they ain't nobody purrfect."

Bay-ed *(Bed)*: "I feel this way 'baout it. He made his bay-ed, so let 'im sleep in hit."

Lecktristy *(Elec-tricity):* "I thank it wuz a feller name of Benjamin Franklin whut faound aout 'bout lecktristy when his Daddy los' patience with him an' tol' him to go fly a kite jus' to git Ben aout o' the haouse."

Cheer *(Chair):* "Jus' hang yore coat on the bak o' thet cheer."

Moanbak *(Come on back):* "Cut th' stirrin' wheel to th' rite an' moanbak."

Dayum *(Damn):* "Frankly, mah deah, I don't giv' a dayum!"

Greeuts *(Grits):* "Pleez pass th' greeuts."

Saar *(Sour):* "Ma, this meeulk tastes lak hit's saar."

Stow *(Store):* "Ah'm goin' to th' stow an' git sum 'baccer. Be rat bak."

Thow *(Throw):* "Thayet uppity ol' Hortense Edwards jus' makes me want to thow up."

Spec *(Expect):* "I rilly wud lak to stay fer supper, but I spec I bes' be gittin' on home."

Sinner *(Center):* "Ol' Charley won th' turkey shoot this mornin'. He flat hit thayet bull's eye dade sinner."

Zat *(Is that):* "This here's my cap. Zat yores?"

War *(Wire):* "I cud fix this thang in nothin' flat if'n I had me a piece o' war."

Zackly *(Exactly):* "Frum Atlanter to Bumminham is zackly 158 miles."

Tawk *(Talk):* "Yeah, I watch TV. But I don't watch none o' them tawk shows."

Sawt *(Salt):* "This here taoun is gonna' miss ol' man Hipple. He was the sawt o' th' earth."

Pitcher *(Picture):* "All right, you young'uns git in th' haouse an' git cleaned up some. We got to go to taoun an' git our pitcher took fer Chrismus."

Phrasin *(Freezing):* "Somebody put some more wood on th' far. It's phrasin' cold in heer."

Shurf *(Sheriff):* "If'n thayet pickup comes by heer jus' one more time a' speedin' I'm gonna' call th' shurf an' hav' 'im locked up."

Ose *(Oldsmobile):* "Did'ja heer that Frankie Bennett traded cars las' week? Traded his '72 Ponyack fer a '79 Ose 88."

Ovair *(Over there):* "I 'prechate th' offer uv a ride but I kin walk. I ain't goin' fur, jus' rite ovair."

Madge *(Marriage):* "Says rat cheer in th' local papuh thayet Ralph Swilley has done ast Mollie Bentley fer her han' in madge."

Abode *(A board):* "I promised the young'uns I wuz gonna' make um a see-saw, but fus I got to see if'n I kin fin' abode."

Tenshun *(Attention):* "All right, class. I want all uv y'all to set up an' pay tenshun."

Venchly *(Eventually):* "Naow then, don't git all upset 'cause we done los' owah fus' 16 ball games. Jus' wuk hard an' don' giv up 'cause we gonna' win a game venchly."

Spishuss *(Suspicious):* "I wudn't git too close to thayet new boy daown th' road if'n I wuz y'all. I bin a' watchin 'im an' he looks spishuss to me."

Skace *(Scarce):* "Wail, Lem, looks lak th' pecan crop is gonna' come up short this yeer. Yessir, pecans is gonna' be skace as hen's teeth."

Po *(Poor):* "Shoot, Roger, you don' know whut bein' po is. They's a fambly ovah in Cedar Creek whut's so po that ever' time they thow a bone out th' bak door th' dog signals fer a fair ketch."

Shaller *(Shallow):* "Yeah, I guess you young'uns kin go in swimmin'—but be shore ya' stay in th' shaller end."

Cutcha *(Cut you):* "One thang 'baout ol' Ben, if'n he gits drunk an' mad at th' same time he'll flat cutcha."

Hesh *(Hush):* "Hesh yo' maouth, boy! Jes' hesh up!"

Mamanem *(Mama and them):* "Howdy, Luke. How's yore mamanem?"

Quair *(Queer):* "I've always sorta' laked ol' Mr. Woods, but he shore has some quair ways, don't he?"

Shivry *(Chivalry):* "Well, thanks fer openin' th' door fer me, Jake. See chillun, th' age o' shivry ain't daid."

Cawk *(Cork):* "Anybody know whut happened to th' cawk stopper whut I had in this syrup bottle?"

Cad *(Carried):* "I cad some peas ovah to Mrs. Nelson lak ya' tol' me to, Pa. She sed thank you."

Skeert *(Scared):* "I'll go fus'. I ain't skeert."

Salary *(Celery):* "Tossed salad jus' ain't tossed salad if'n it don't hav sum salary in it."

Less *(Let's):* "Less go to th' ball game an' then go git a Big Mac."

Loud *(Allowed):* "Mama said we wuzn't loud to go to taoun atter dark."

Foe (Four): "I ain't memrized it all yet, but I know how it starts off . . . "Foe sco an' sebum years ago . . ."

Fussed (First): "Yes, m'am, I know th' answer! Th' fussed man whut walked on th' moon wuz Neil Armstrong."

Doe (Door): "Somebody open th' doe! I got a armload o' stovewood."

Astor (Ask her): "I rilly don' thank Ma's gonna' lemmee go, but I'll astor."

Menshun (Mention): "When ya' git to th' front doe, jus' menshun mah name an' you'll git a good seat."

Nudder (Another): "Mama, kin I hav nudder piece o'cake?"

Leckshun (election): "Can't buy no likker today, Henry. It's leckshun day. Can't nobody but th' politicians git drunk."

Pleese (Police): "Mus' be havin' trouble daoun at th' juke joint. I seen two pleese cars go by."

Lane (Laying): "I ain't worked none since I got laid off in Janawerry, but I'm goin' to wuk nex' week fer a haouse bilder lane tile."

Yistitty (Yesterday): "I gotta' go bak to DEE-troit in the' mornin'. I come in on th' bus late yistitty evenin'."

Rail (Real): "I seen Mr. Sullivan daoun at th' pig sale this mornin' an' I thot he looked rail good."

Blong (Belong): "I don't wanna' go to Sally Mae's birthday party. I jus' don't feel lak I blong there."

Paytrotick *(Patriotic):*
"One o' th' thangs I like bes' 'baout the Foth of July prade is the paytrotick music them bans play."

Sammitch *(Sandwich):*
"No, thank ya' m'am, I done et. Mama fixed me a bloney an' 'mater sammitch."

Tar *(Tire):*
"Weeda' bin here 'fore naow but we had a flat tar jus' aoutside o' Waycross."

Wangs *(Wings):*
"Oh yeah? Well, if'n a frog had wangs he wudn't keep a' bumpin his tail on th' groun."

Ax *(Ask):*
"Jus' set there, Ned, an' don't ax so many questions."

Bail *(Bell):*
"We bettuh hurry up. I thank I jes' heered th' skool bail rang."

Ball *(Boil):*
"Can she cook? Heck, thet ol' gal cudn't ball watah 'thout scorchin' it."

Cane Chew *(Can't you):*
"Cane chew jus' see ol' Bobby Jack all decked aout in one o' them monkey suits fer his sister's weddin'?"

Legible *(Eligible):*
"Ain't no way Booger Creek kin win thet football game t'nite 'cause the qwatahbak ain't legible. He flunked Ainglish an' Hist'ry."

Coat *(Court):*
"I guess we won't be a' seein' much of ol' Jay Bridges fer the nex' few yeers. He got sentenced to eight yeers in Circus Coat this mornin'."

Empire *(Umpire):*
"Them Atlanter Braves shore got th' shawt end o' the stick agin' them Chicargo Cubs yistitty, did'n they? That fus' base empire flat missed thet play on Murphy at fus' base. He wuz safe by two steps."

Tuck *(Took):*   "I ain't never tuck a drink o' likker in muh life."

So much for the vocabulary. There are a couple of other tricks of the redneck trade that, if mastered, will prove invaluable to you in communicating with your new neighbors. These are cardinal rules of redneck grammar and musts for proper Redneck speech:

- Never pronounce the "g" in words endin' with "ing."
- No matter if you're talkin' baout man, woman, child, a haoun' dog, or a pickup truck, put "ol" in front.
- Always put the accent or emphasis on the first syllable of words with two or more. For instance: DEE-troit, UM-breller; IN-shorance; and JU-ly.

And just as a bonus, here's a great redneck line for you to store in your memory bank for future use. It is sure to melt a redneck girlfriend's heart:

"You jus' 'member this, Sugah, Long's I got a biscuit, you got half."

Sorta' chokes a feller up, don't it?

REDNECKS OUGHT TO BE PROUD OF THEIR DRAWL

In my travels 'roun th' New Nited States ovah th' pass 30 years, 'specially mah years o' confinement in th' nawth, fornirs repeatedly made fun of th' way I talk, 'specially them Noo Yawkers.

I tried f'r yeers t'make bleevers uvem but they jus' ain't no way. They boun' an' d'termin t' keep on livin' in littyrate darkness, spite my efforts t'edjukate 'em. 'Nother thang. Whut makesum s'dang shor they talk rite? They cud be in f'r a heckuva shock cum Judgmint Day. Ain't nobody never rilly prooved t'me that God talks nawthen. In fack, I fin' it plumb hard t'bleev He's gonna' wekkom me at th' gate with a "Hi, guy! Welcome aboard! And treat yourself to the hors d' oeuvres."

I'd druther bleeve He'll shake an' say, "Hey! How y'all?! C'mon in an' make y'self t' home! Greeits n' biskitts 'bout done. Jus' take out an' hep y'sef."

WRITING LIKE WE TALK

Nother thang. I ham't figgered outchet why people don't write lak they talk. Lemme' giv' ya' a hyperthettical sitchiation an' see if'n ya' git whut I mean.

Jus' suppos'n Robbie Nell Bell (Robbie Nail Bail), fum Almer, jus' happen t'meet Gaylord Throckmorton III, from Brooklyn, N.Y., in th' Waycross bus station an' they taken a likin' t'one 'nother an' all. An' jus' suppos'n Robbie Nail wuz so strucken by Gaylord that she wrote him a letter, lak she talks. Here's whut ol' Gaylord might try t' read:

Dere Gay-Lord

I wuz praoud t'meet up witcha' in Waycross an' I'm prad ar paths crost. I kep tellin' Mommer and Popper that if'n I travel'd 'nuff I'd fin' a mayen lak you. I nebber mayet no mayen whut helt my hayend right off and y' mighta noticed I swallered hard. I jus' knowed they had t' be a mayen somers f'r me an' I bleeve you're him, Gay-Lord. Rilly, I thank mebbe weuz made f'r one 'nother, lak I tode ya' in th' cafe 'tween buses.

T'be troofle, I bin rail p'ticklar 'bout who I got innersted in but just feel lak you a rail nice bawy whut hannle's hissef' wail.

I c'mon home after you lef' an' thot 'bout you holdin' mah hayend an' acourse that mayed mah faingers taingle an' all. I know ya' prolly seen my sweatin' a heap but that won't fum th' hot coffy 'er nothin like thayat. Ituz jus' thayat I ain't nebber rilly bin 'roun much an' don' a whol lotta' han-holdin' 'er nothin' to be 16—goin' on 17.

This mornin' I tol' Popper 'bout you an' he figgers you ar prolly a'rite, eben bein' from Noo Yawk an' all. An' he kep on askin' whayre Brooklyn wuz at. I tol' im 'bout the breeidge up thayre I read 'bout in school an' he grunted. Popper has this ole thang 'bout gruntin' wheun he's all through talkin', er listnin', so I queeit.

I thank ya' fer th' meeulkshake an' th' card witcher pitcher on it. Mommer don' lak th' beard and Popper is a' havin' trouble figurin' aout why come you're wearin' a earring if'n you're a bawy lak I tol' em you wuz. (Y'ar a bawy, aint'cha Gay-Lord?)

I be stoppin' fr naow but I'll mail this in the mawnin' 'fo I ketch th' bus fo' grammuh school. It shore wuz goodt' meetcha an' I'll be watchin' reglar fo' a lettuh fum ya'. Rat naow I got t' study my histry 'cause Popper jus' grunted.

Yores truly, Robbie Nell.

I'd give three yards of chitlins and a dozen pickled pig's feet to sit and watch Gaylord try and read Robbie Nell's letter.

A few years ago the good people in Chattanooga, Tennessee, got riled up when a meddlin' Yankee woman with a college degree and a title tried to change the way Chattanoogians talk. She offered a course on how people could get ahead by abandoning their southern accent.

When I heard about the hollerin' up there, I called my good friend Robbie Nell Bell from Alma. "Robbie," I asked her, "do you have any people like that in Alma?"

"Shoot naw!" she replied. "Ain't but one furrin' car in taoun an' it b'longs to a Yankee fortune teller named Madame T'ressir."

"Oh? Where'd she come from?" I asked.

"Danged if I know. Some lil' ol' town up close to C'lumbyar, Saouth C'liner," she told me. "Folks 'raound cheer don't trust 'er, neether."

"Why is that?"

"Wail, my mommer says it's cause she don't eat greeutz or chitlins, totes a big ol' pocketbook over her shoulder an' wears shoes in th' summertime," Robbie Nail allowed. "An' I know Mayel don' lack her a tall cause he thowed her outta' his juke 'baout three weeks ago when she prissed in lack somebody rail special an' ordered ice coffee. I tell ya', newspaper man, that flat didn' cut it with Mayel 'cause he's rail patrotic an' flat don't put up with nothin' un-'Murkin like some Yankee woman orderin' ice coffee in his juke joint. Way he figgers it tha's daounright Commonist, baout lack hot tea in the Huddle House or that keesh stuff in Lil's Cafe an' Beauty Shop in Baxley. 'Sides, Mayel's got a C'nfedrate flag in th' back winder of his pickup, a tattoo of the New Nited States flag on his lef' arm up nex' t' his heart, an' he b'longs to th' 'Murkin Leegun in Douglas. He jus' showed her th' sign whut hangs over the juke box: "We Reserve The Right To Refuse Service To Anyone Whut Don't Act Right", an' tol' her to git los'."

"What'd she do then?"

"She picked up her big ol' pocketbook, slung that sucker over her shoulder, yailled somethin' furrin' at

Mayel, got in her li'l ol' car an' hauled buggy. Man! She thowed gravel slam up on top o' th' buildin' when she took off. An' ol' Mayel was jus' a hollerin' at her, 'Same to ya', Yankee!' an' Madam T'ressir ain't bin back since. An' I kin tail ya' this, good buddy, we ain't missed 'er none."

The more I thought about it, the more I agreed with Emory University English professor Lee Pederson.

"Drawl-busting is a very dangerous undertaking. When you start messing with your speech, it's like the idiots who mess with the environment; no one knows what will happen for a long time. It might be like a sex-change operation—irreversible. You're culturally neutered."

And consider this. Supposin' you were to take that class. Then one day a deputy sheriff in Ludowici pulls you over and your voice doesn't match up with the Tennessee tag? What then? Might get arrested for car theft or, worse, impersonating a Yankee. One thing for sure, he'd be in a "heap o' trouble, boy."

I have to go along with my friend Ludlow Porch, who said in all his wisdom following a brief visit to New York City. "I'm thoroughly convinced that the most effective birth control device there is a New York accent."

So Southerners, it's time to be proud of the way we talk!

THE BARE REDNECK NECESSITIES

In order that I may be of all possible assistance in effecting a smooth transition from North to South, it is imperative that certain basic items readily identifiable with the redneck lifestyle be purchased prior to departure. The mere possession of them will project the desired image upon arrival. It stands to reason that some items cannot be purchased in the North but every effort should be made to obtain them shortly after arrival in the Southland, or on the way down.

Some of the necessary items can be purchased as far north as Kentucky and Maryland. Some can be ordered from Sears and Roebuck, as well as L. L. Bean. Leave no stone unturned to complete the checklist and familiarize yourself with each item as quickly as possible.

Save the list and check off each item as it is obtained.

- Used pickup truck, with muffler and tailpipe dragging.
- One or two dogs of questionable pedigree.
- One 4 x 6 Confederate flag.
- One black cap with a yellow CAT Diesel patch.
- One belt buckle no smaller than a large pizza.
- One Army fatigue jacket with insignia removed.
- One 30.06 rifle, with scope; and one Remington Model 1100 .12 gauge shotgun. Hang both in rear window of pickup.
- Install tape player in pickup and purchase an ample supply of country music tapes, preferably by Willie Nelson, Hank Williams, Jr., Johnny Cash, "Alabama," Merle Haggard, Ricky Skaggs, David Allen Coe and Earl Thomas Conley.

• At least three Wrangler western shirts, with snaps.

• A week's supply of white socks, maybe two pair.

• An ample supply of jeans, preferably Levis.

• This is optional, but if you really want to go all out, get yourself a tattoo. The very sight of it will answer a lot of questions and open a lot of redneck doors. Two of the more popular ones are, "M-O-T-H-E-R" done in navy blue and centered in a rose pink heart on the upper left arm, and "DEATH BEFORE DISHONOR" wrapped around a dagger on the right forearm. (These can easily be obtained in either Atlantic City or Newark.)

Caution: It is strongly suggested that you refrain from having your wife or girlfriend's name or initials tattoed any place on your body. Just remember when considering same, it's a fact that a tattoo is very permanent while wives and girlfriends of rednecks ain't.

• Two or three pictures of horses and pelicans painted on black velvet. County fairs are the best source for these, and the artist will paint them while you wait. Average cost: $4.75. And buy a small light to hang over the pictures, for effect.

• Levi Garrett chewing tobacco is a must. If you don't chew and can't spit without soiling the front of your shirt and chin, by all means learn how. A redneck without Levi Garrett is like Buckingham Palace without a throne. (Buckingham Palace is in London. London is in England. England is "over

yonder," somewheres.)

• At least two ashtrays mounted on the backs of plastic horses; one for the den and one for the bedroom. These can be picked up at the county fair at the same time the pictures are purchased. Just knock over a few weighted milk bottles, throw enough coins in evasive saucers or bust enough balloons with "three-for-a-dollar" darts and you've got 'em. Plan to spend about $19 per ash tray. Remember, the folks what run them concessions ain't runnin' 'em for charity.

• One Timex watch with a broken crystal. This is strong and convincing evidence that you are a working man or fight a lot, either being in your favor.

• One Zippo cigarette lighter. And get in the habit of keeping it in the watch pocket of your Levis. Never light a female redneck's cigarette with it. That would be a dead giveaway that you are a pretender to the redneck world. Hand it to her and let

her light her own cigarette. And be dang sure she returns it.

• A belt with your first name or initials burned in the back of it. This is instant status.

• One wallet-size photograph of each of your children, I mean the ones presently living with you. Rednecks always pull out the pictures of the kids when they get drunk, and rednecks do show their kids' pictures a lot. Following the photo exhibition they all gather around the bar and sing religious songs. "In the Garden" is a big favorite. If you don't know all the words, learn 'em.

• One boat paddle. Never mind that you don't own a boat. A paddle in the back of a '73 Chevy pickup speaks for itself.

• Finally, be sure there is always a copy of National Enquirer on the dash of the pickup. Rednecks, especially redneck women, believe the junk that's in it.

REDNECKS ARE THE ULTIMATE AUTHORITY

There are certain things that you just don't learn in school. You just learn about them from experience, or from your mama and daddy. Rednecks consider themselves the ultimate authority on some of these things, and they don't back off an inch when it comes time to tell you they are.

Rednecks are self-proclaimed authorities on:

- Huntin'
- Fishin'
- Football
- Baseball
- Basketball
- Turkey shoots
- Country music
- Barbequin'
- Beer
- Pickup trucks
- Frog giggin'
- Hog killin'
- Stock car racin'
- Rasslin'
- Women
- Automobile and truck repairs
- Whittlin'
- Whistlin'
- Guitar pickin'
- Tobacco chewin'
- Truck drivin'
- Poker
- Crap shootin'
- Moonshine
- Cane grindin'
- Candy pullin'
- Square dancin'
- Tree cuttin'
- Tractor pullin'
- Deer skinnin'
- Pool shootin'
- Arm rasslin'
- Milkin' cows
- Ropin' steers
- Killin' rattlesnakes
- Wasp nests
- Rivers
- Motorcycles
- The Grand Ole Opry
- Grits
- Syrup
- Country ham
- Pot likker
- Banana puddin'
- Iced tea
- Blue jeans
- Belts
- Western hats
- Cigarettes
- Wine
- Pocket knives

SECTION TWO

REDNECK RATIONS

... OR GOURMET COOKING IN DIXIELAND

GRITS ARE STILL KING IN DIXIE

For generations people living outside the confines of the South have labored under the misapprehension that "Cotton is King" in Dixie. Let us put such false information to rest once and for all. Grits reign as king in Dixie.

Grits are almost a way of life in my native Georgia, with the exception of Atlanta where Yankee refugees have succeeded in teaching the natives to eat potatoes and English muffins for breakfast. And I say that any man who eats potatoes and English muffins for breakfast will eat quiche, and do other unmanly things.

I served in the South Pacific during World War II with a true son of the South, Will Brinson. Will was born and raised on a farm in South Georgia. He was proud of his heritage and was never one to compromise his beliefs. This trait reared its proud head one morning after Will had been assigned to a patrol destined to seek out and capture Japanese in the hills north of Manila in the Philippine Islands.

Will approached the Captain. He asked to speak to him in private. His request was granted and the two men stepped behind a latrine. It didn't take Will long to come right to the point. Speaking up, he said, "Captain, if it's all the same to you I'd rather not be John Bubenski's partner on patrol this mornin'."

"Why not, Brinson?" asked the Captain. "I think Bubenski's a good man."

"Well, sir, he don't eat grits, an' I find it awful hard to trust a man whut don't eat grits," was his reply.

Actually, I guess I felt quite the same way. I was born and raised in South Georgia, too, and I never in my life saw anybody eat potatoes for breakfast until I was inducted into the U.S. Army.

The main problem Yankees have with grits is that (1) they don't know how to cook 'em and (2) they don't know how to eat 'em. It's as simple as that.

A good ol' redneck or his redneck wife can cook up a pot of grits before you can say "Aunt Jemima." And they'll be delicious, too. But I'll be the first to admit that grits are a little bland unless prepared right.

Instant grits won't get the job done. Neither will grits that come packaged ten to a box. They're called "flow-thru boil-in-bag" grits. I can halfway understand flow-thru tea bags by Lipton, but I ain't ready for no flow-thru grits by nobody.

You need real grits straight from the mill, and you boil them suckers until they're ready. You can tell when its time. My mama would never serve a grit before its time. Grits sorta' creep out of the pot when the time comes, like a bird dog creeping up on a quail.

Once on the plate, grits should be crowned with a big dab of real butter and sprinkled generously with salt and pepper. Then, if you like, you can chop up your bacon or sausage in 'em— and do the same thing with your eggs. Just mix the whole concoction together, and then add more salt and pepper. Then, you try to make the whole thing come out even with your toast or biscuits.

Of course, the kids can have a lot of fun with grits, too. They can play like it's snowing down in Dixie and, when the grits get a little cool, build a grits snowman. Or they can take their forks and carve little trenches in the grits, pour ham gravy in them and watch it run like rainwater in a drainage ditch. Maybe make grits snowballs when mama and daddy ain't in the room.

Lukewarm grits are also great for making grits castles and forts. With a good imagination and a plate filled with leftover grits, the possibilities are endless.

Sure beats the heck out of trying to work with luke-warm hashbrowns. . . .

◆　◆　◆　◆　◆

In his book, *Kiss My Grits!* Roy Overcast has some wonderful grits recipes. Six of my favorites are here:

Grits for Good Friends

1½ cup quick grits
4 cups water
1 teaspoon salt
½ cup butter or
  margarine
6 ounces garlic cheese
  spread
4 ounces grated Swiss
  cheese

½ cup milk
1 cup sour cream
3 eggs, beaten
Salt and pepper to taste
⅓ cup grated Parmesan
  cheese
Paprika

Preheat oven to 325°. Bring salted water to a boil and stir in grits. Add butter, garlic and Swiss cheeses, mixing thoroughly until cheeses melt. Let cool. Combine milk, sour cream, beaten eggs, salt and pepper to taste into grits mixture. Pour mixture into a greased casserole. Sprinkle top with Parmesan cheese and paprika. Bake at 325° for 1 hour. Serves 8.

Fried Grits

1 cup quick grits
4 cups water
2 teaspoons salt

1 cup flour
1 egg, beaten
Bacon grease

Bring salted water to a boil and stir in grits. Cook on low heat for 10 minutes, stirring frequently. Pour into tubes (glasses, cans or canning glasses can be used) and chill for a few hours (or overnight). Before serving: cut into ½-inch slices, dip into egg, flour and brown in a skillet with bacon grease. Serves 8.

Fantastic Grits

1 cup grits
1 stick butter or mar-
  garine
1 roll garlic cheese

1 egg, beaten
¾ cup cream
Corn chips

Preheat oven at 350°. Cook grits as directed. Add butter, cheese, egg and cream, making sure cheese melts thoroughly and stirring so cream won't curdle. Pour mixture into a greased casserole. Crush corn chips and cover top of mixture. Bake at 350° for 45 minutes. Serves 8.

Lilly's Tennessee Grits

½ cup water
1 teaspoon salt
2 cups quick grits

4 tablespoons butter
  or margarine
2 tablespoons milk

Bring salted water to a boil and quickly stir in grits. Cover for 1 minute on medium heat. Grits will be thick, add butter. To dilute add 2 tablespoons of milk. Continue to cook until thick and creamy. Serve with Tennessee Country Ham and red-eye gravy. Serves 4.

Louisiana Grits

2 tablespoons bacon
  grease
2 tablespoons flour
½ cup finely chopped
  onions
1 medium chopped
  green pepper

½ cup finely chopped
  celery
1 cup quick grits
3 fresh tomatoes, peeled
  and chopped
1 cup crumbled bacon

Heat bacon grease in skillet and gradually add flour, stirring constantly until mixture becomes a light brown. Add chopped onion, green pepper and celery and cook for 5 minutes. Cook grits as directed and add to mixture, then add tomatoes and crumbled bacon. Pour into casserole and top with crumbled bacon. Serves 6.

Florida Grits

½ cup water
1 teaspoon salt
½ cup grits
1 can shrimp chowder
1 cup milk

½ cup grated cheddar
  cheese
4 tablespoons butter
  or margarine
2 dozen boiled shrimp

Bring salted water to a boil and stir in grits. Cover and cook for 2 minutes. Stir in half of milk and cheese. Cover and cool for 1 minute. Stir in rest of milk and butter and shrimp chowder; blend well. Continue to cook on medium heat until thick and creamy (milk makes grits creamy). Lay shrimp on top and bake for 40 minutes at 375°. Serves 6.

YANKEE MEETS REDNECK OVER LUNCH

WHO EATS HUSHPUPPIES WITH A FORK!?!

I know of nothing more refreshing than having lunch with a pretty girl. And I don't cull 'em, neither. Age is no factor. Neither is nativity. This was verified as recently as last week when I invited a Yankee girl, Nancy, a recent arrival in Dublin, to have lunch with me. Well, she's almost a Yankee. She's from Michigan, but that ain't like being from New York or New Jersey where the pedigreed and bonafide Yankees hail from.

We were about halfway through our salads before we broke the sound barrier and reached the point where each of us could understand what the other was saying. And there is a difference, you know.

Like, I say "sirrup," and she says "seerrup." I say "pah," and she says "pye." I say "wawffles," and she says "wahffles." I say "DEE-troyt," and she says "D'troit." I say "Ponyack," and she says, "Pahntiac." And on and on. But, Nancy'll learn to talk right if she hangs around native Georgians like me long enough.

TRYING TO BE ONE OF THE BUNCH

I have to admire Nancy for making an effort to blend in with us here in Georgia. You know, "When in Rome. . . ."

I watched as she scanned the menu, and was pleased when she ordered catfish. Me? I ordered Southern fried chicken. No surprise. I *always* order Southern fried chicken. One of these days I'm gonna' order Northern fried chicken. That would be like ordering an Eastern omelette, right?

49

Nancy and I chatted while awaiting the arrival of our food. I learned that she likes Dublin, and that a friend in her apartment building, Gay, had forewarned her about having lunch with me, advising her not to do it.

By and by, our food arrived and I squared off against my Southern fried chicken while Nancy stared long and hard at her catfish—and hushpuppies, which she didn't understand.

"What are these? Corn fritters?" she asked as she rolled a hushpuppy around on her plate with her fork.

"They're hushpuppies," I told her. "Some people call them corn dodgers."

"Oh," was her only reply.

Shortly, I was up to my elbows in Southern fried chicken, but I watched with keen interest as Nancy played "roll the hushpuppy," and finally reached for her knife. And . . . you ain't gonna' believe this:

She actually began carving into the hushpuppy with the knife and spearing the little pieces with her fork!

A waitress dropped a pot of coffee. A fella' at the counter got choked on a biscuit. And a man at the table adjacent to ours sud-denly became petrified, finally commenting to his luncheon companion, "Jack, I've been overseas, fought the Japanese, eaten all kinds of food, and devoured wood alcohol. But I'll be danged if I ever saw anybody eat hushpuppies with a fork."

Jack peered over his glasses, continued to gnaw on a chicken leg, and grunted, "Hmmmm . . . mus' be a Yankee, or a furriner."

Next came the catfish, and Nancy attacked the little fella' in the same manner as she had the hushpuppy, with knife and fork. And I eyed the piece of corn on the cob that rested on her plate.

Nancy obviously sensed that I was watching, along with several others. "What's the matter? Haven't you seen anyone eat with a knife and fork before?" she asked.

"Well," she asked, "how do you eat catfish and hushpuppies?"

"Same way I eat fried chicken, with my hands," I said. "And how do you eat fried chicken?"

"Same way I eat catfish and hushpuppies, with a knife and fork," she said. "And you know something else?"

"What?"

"Gay was right!"

As we were leaving I couldn't help but overhear this exchange between a waitress and Jack.
". . . and I'll bet she don't eat grits, neither."

"You got that right. Them things are hard to handle with a knife and fork."

Nancy had her own perspective on what it's like to come south to the promised land.

CAN ANYONE HELP THIS GOOD OL' GIRL?

I'm the girl who eats hushpuppies with a fork. Yup, hushpuppies, catfish, fried chicken and even barbecued ribs. I didn't think Bo was the kind of fella to eat and tell!

So, you can imagine my excitement when I read Bo's headline, "How can Yankees blend in with southern living?" At last, I thought, I can learn from the master himself how I can fit right in and be a Southerner like you guys (that's Yankee for "y'all").

Well, if you read further than the headline, you know that Bo's tips for transplanted Yankees are geared toward the male species. North or South, I'm not going to trade in my Michigan winter-rusted Chevy for a pickup with a gunrack, wear T-shirts with gross sayings, or learn to spit. No way. Not ever.

Why no tips for women trying to assimilate in the South?

Are you discriminating against women again, "Bozo?" How about some info for us prospective good ol' girls?

MY PROBLEMS BEGIN AT "THE PIG"

When I considered moving South I thought my biggest adjustments would be to the climate and the dialect. Little did I know that the grocery store would be the twilight zone for me.

Can anyone explain to me the differences in the seemingly hundreds of varieties of cornmeal? In Detroit there were two kinds, Aunt Jemima and the store's brand, both yellow and stoneground. I was therefore dumbfounded when I came upon a vast array of cornmeal at Piggly Wiggly. There was cornmeal and cornmeal

mix, yellow, white, sifted, fine, coarse, stoneground, waterground. And then there were about a million different brand names.

I felt very ignorant, and I'm sure I had a puzzled look on my face, as I read the little packages as if they were pages of a novel I couldn't put down.

But my inspection paid off. I found that Jiffy Corn Muffin Mix was by far the best. It was made in Michigan, like me!

And what about grits? I've never eaten them because no one can actually tell me what they are or how to fix them. A cookbook I received for Christmas, "A Taste of Georgia," has three recipes for grits. One calls for eggs and cheese, the second has Tabasco sauce and garlic, and the third is a simple recipe submitted by Mrs. Billy Carter that calls for grits, water, milk and salt, and is cooked for up to five hours. And just today I heard of a recipe for shrimp and grits.

Shrimp?!

Asked what grits are like, many people have told me they're like Cream of Wheat hot cereal. Now, *that* I'm familiar with because Mom used to fortify us with it on cold, snowy mornings. But the thought of Cream of Wheat with eggs and cheese and Tabasco and garlic or shrimp is disgusting! And if you cook Cream of Wheat for five hours you'll end up with nothing but a substance suitable for patching a roof and a pan that will never come clean.

Serve me grits and I'll try them, but as far as I'm concerned right now, grits are newspapers little boys sell door-to-door to earn money or they're the annoying particles that Ajax leaves in the bathtub.

Fatback? I don't know what it is but my arteries close up just thinking about it.

Then there are the things that both Yankees and Southerners eat but call by *different names.*

I drink pop, sometimes *Coke.* You guys call all pop "Coke." That's very confusing to me. I know you'd understand me if I asked for soda, but up north a soda has ice cream in it and I'm liable to be real disappointed if I order a soda and just get pop.

Parched peanuts are what I know as roasted or ballpark peanuts. And boiled peanuts, I've found, should be avoided. (Unless they're Griffin's Gourmet Microwave Peanuts, of course!)

ONE IMPORTANT DIFFERENCE

Yankees who have traveled through or lived in the South think Southern hospitality can't be beat. And I couldn't agree more. In my 26 years in Michigan I never experienced such friendliness, kindness, and genuine concern for people as I have here in the South.

I may not be a good ol' girl yet, but I sure hope someday to be as sweet as you guys. I mean y'all. I'm catching on.

EATING OUT IS A WAY OF LIFE

Eating out is a time-honored tradition in the Deep South. And any excuse will do. But we're not talking here about calling Pierre's for reservations and downing canapes, Maine lobster, oysters on the half-shell, chateaubriand, rare roast beef, chocolate mousse or key lime pie. Not on your life. What we're talkin' here is real roll up your sleeves, take out and help yourself, eatin'.

We're talkin' things like cane grindings, peanut boilings, candy pullings, bird suppers, dove suppers, fish fries and barbeques. (I had best explain the difference here and now between bird suppers and dove suppers because any aspiring redneck will be expected to attend such outings and it is a must that he know the difference.)

When an invitation is extended in Georgia for an individual to attend a BIRD supper, the bird served will be quail. But true sons of the south just say "bird" supper, meaning quail.

On the other hand, if the supper is to be a minor league affair and doves are to be served the person extending the invitation will say "dove" supper.

In either event, you can be assured of one thing; grits will be served at both affairs.

You can also rest assured that music will usually be provided, either by a local group who just like to pick and sing or by a fellow with a guitar who will play at the drop of a biscuit.

In most cases, the affairs are "men only" shindigs. But in a weak moment the women are invited to maybe one or two a year. When this happens the men usually wind up in the yard after supper talking about such things as football, the weather (too much rain, or

54

not enough), and politics and money (or the lack of it).

Meanwhile, the women folks gather inside and discuss things like school, their old man's job, "The Young and the Restless," "General Hospital," "Dallas," and "People's Court."

On rare occasions when the younguns are present they run, jump, climb, fall down, stump their toes, and cry. Just a fun time for all.

Of course, there's always the village joke-teller who repeats the same jokes at every outing and laughs louder than anybody. He wouldn't miss one if he had to slip out of Intensive Care to get there.

One thing about rednecks, they love to share.

Another thing, suppers are big in any election year. While the good ol' boys may not know who's running for office, they can sure as heck tell you what's on the menu.

Probably the most popular food spread in the South is "dinner on the grounds," well known to all country boys. There is usually more food left over than most restaurants prepare.

A good friend, Ludlow Porch of Atlanta, is a self-proclaimed "dinner on the grounds" food expert. He backs up to no one when it comes to what he calls denominational cooking, and his expertise in the field comes from having "pigged out" at many such church dinners. Here's what Porch has to say on the subject:

● "The Methodists are far and away the best string-bean cooks on the face of the earth."

- "If you want fried chicken the way God intended, then you must eat fried chicken prepared by a Baptist. Nobody, but nobody, can fry a chicken like a Baptist."
- "Church of Christ women make the best corn bread."
- "Presbyterians make the best rolls."
- "Episcopalians are particularly adept at hams and roasts."
- "Catholic goods tend to be spicy, and smell of garlic, but taste great—for days."
- "Free-will Baptists have no equal when it comes to cooking chocolate layer cake, lemon pies and banana pudding."
- "The common denominator regarding denominational cooking seems to be in the iced tea. They almost all like it sweetened, with real sugar. I can therefore reach only one conclusion: If you like your iced tea unsweetened, you better get right with the Lord 'cause based on the evidence in question I tend to think you're in a bunch of trouble."

◆   ◆   ◆   ◆   ◆

In addition to iced tea, many rednecks have this thing about buttermilk. Frankly, I love a good cold glass of buttermilk but I have one abiding concern about drinking it and that is this:

I always wonder, after drinking a glass of buttermilk, if my stomach looks like the glass does after the buttermilk dries.

It's food for thought.

THESE CAFES SHOULD HAVE BEEN ON SOMEBODY'S LIST

If you're looking for a good redneck eatin' place, you shouldn't waste your time hangin' around any restaurants. Redneck eatin' is done at juke joints and cafes. What's the difference? Simple. A cafe is a small restaurant. And that's as much as any self-respecting redneck will concede to the people who wear neckties during the week.

I grew up with cafes. Restaurants were way off in big cities like Dublin, Waycross and Waynesboro when I lived as a boy in such hamlets as Scott, Dudley and Vidette before moving to Alma, where I met my first cafe. Cafeteria? Perish the thought. I'd heard about one named Morrison's in Savannah and another, the S and S, in Macon. But surely they were for the affluent, those privileged few who had such 1930s luxuries as car radios and white sidewall tires.

First time I ever ate in a cafe? Sure I remember it. It was in Alma at Tapley's cafe when my daddy's younger brother came to visit one Sunday all the way from Douglas. The menu? It was written on a blackboard behind the counter. Made sense to me. Run out of pork chops, butterbeans or biscuits and Mrs. Tapley just erased 'em. Life was so much simpler back then.

I learned from the experience that eating in a cafe presents serious problems, though. Like when you ate Sunday dinner in a cafe there was no cold chicken or ham and biscuit in the safe or under the cloth on the dinner table in mid-afternoon. When you're through eating dinner in a cafe, baby, you're through until supper and that's a heck of a long time to wait when you're an eight-year old accustomed to eating at least three or four times between dinner and supper.

After Alma, our next move was to Oglethorpe but I gave all my cafe business to Montezuma because that's where Hamby's Cafe was. One day somebody will probably write a book about Hamby's Cafe and get rich. Meanwhile, here's a short story about it.

I was 12 when we moved to Oglethorpe. The only picture show was two miles away in Montezuma. So was Hamby's Cafe.

A quarter would get you two hamburgers (five cents each) and a Coke (five cents) at Hamby's. The remaining dime got you in the picture show right down the street. Here was the plan every Saturday: walk to Montezuma, go to Hamby's, eat a hamburger and drink a Coke; buy another hamburger loaded down with onions and stick it inside your shirt before going to the picture show.

Oooohhh, those Hamby's hamburgers were delicious! They were about the size of a syrup bucket lid and as thin as an OCB cigarette paper before we loaded 'em up with mustard, catsup, pickles and onions, and onions, and onions. I'd flat give a

five dollar bill for one right now. No, make that a ten dollar bill for two.

I never knew her first name. Nobody did. We just knew her as Ma Holder and she ran Holder's Cafe in Lumpkin, my next stop after four years and oodles of Hamby's hamburgers.

Holder's was unique. Well, I don't know if that's exactly the right word. Maybe it was unusual. No: original. That's the word. Holder's was original.

It was located next to Clyde Richardson's store. I worked at Mr. Clyde's on Saturdays. I worked there so I could eat dinner and supper (lunch and dinner was for them affluent's) at Holder's cafe with his sons, Bobby and Clyde, Jr. Best I can recall, I made $2.00 working at the store and went home broke when the store closed on Saturday night. Ma Holder had my pay. That's o.k. I had her homemade pie, etc.

Remember oilcloth? Ma Holder's tables were covered with red-checkered oilcloth. Fancy. Her daughters, Margaret and Mary, had aprons to match. Remember when waitresses wore aprons? Margaret and Mary wore clean red-checkered aprons. Ma saw to that. Hers was white. She did the cooking.

Today, Ma Holder's would be a restaurant, but in 1942–43 it was a cafe. Somehow, I can't visualize her establishment as a restaurant. She sure served good groceries.

Another eating place that holds fond memories for me is long gone. Remember the Pig n' Whistle in Macon? How could I ever forget it? I kissed a girl for the first time in the parking lot there between pigs. Our faces were so greasy I slid slap up to her right eyebrow on that initial attempt.

Then, there's The Varsity in Athens. Memories, many memories. That's where I proposed somewhere between an order of fries and a chocolate shake while Ted Weems whistled "Heartaches." She said yes and I ran like a scared rabbit. I haven't been back since. Too dangerous.

Then there was The Mimosa in Baxley, The Pig in Jesup (best barbeque this side of hog heaven), Mrs. Wynn's in Lyons, Mrs. Ricks' in Soperton (leave hungry and it was your fault). Dasher's near Blitchton had great fish and The Station in Metter was equally as good.

These were all cafes. Not a restaurant in the bunch. I sorta' grew up with 'em. The Nic-Nac in Statesboro got me through college. I'd have starved without it.

I'd hate to have to vote in a "Best Cafe" contest with such entries to choose from. Only one I could eliminate would be The Varsity in Athens. I got the livin' daylights scared out of me there.

So, what's the difference between a cafe and a restaurant? I guess it depends on who's buyin'.

RECIPES THAT TOUCH A REDNECK'S HEART

I doubt that there is anything more pleasing to the ear of a Southern cook than the sound of a good grunt or burp at the end of a meal. Both are symbolic of her man's appreciation for a job well done in the kitchen.

Of course, the men take understandable pride in their ability to cook up a great meal, especially when it comes to cooking wild game and unusual dishes. And they will eat anything that can't outfly or outrun them. Chitlins? That's another story altogether.

Just a few of the delectable dishes prepared by redneck men, particularly at "men only" suppers at a camphouse, are baked possum and coon, squirrel and catfish mull; deep-fried turtle, alligator and rattlesnake, fried fish with corn dodgers or hushpuppies (one and the same), deep-fried mountain oysters (bull testicles), venison, dove or quail. All, of course, are served with grits and iced tea.

But, there are certain dishes at which the women folks excel. Just one visit to a homecoming, a family reunion or a church dinner-on-the-grounds will substantiate that. Actually, these events are nothing more than contests, with each lady doing her dead-level best to prepare the one dish that everybody in attendance says is the best on the table.

Here are eleven of the most popular Southern recipes that any true redneck would leave a poker game to eat;

Old Fashioned Hoecake Bread Inez

2 cups self-rising flour	¼ cup shortening
1 teaspoon baking powder	¾ cup buttermilk

In large mixing bowl, mix flour, baking powder, shortening and buttermilk with fork. Roll dough onto floured surface and flatten. Drop into skillet filled to ¼-inch depth with oil and fry until golden brown on both sides.

It is the considered opinion of most rednecks that the good Lord intended that hoecake bread be eaten with sugar cane syrup, torn off and sopped in a counter-clockwise manner.

—Inez Hanna

Buttermilk Biscuits

2½ cups flour	3 tablespoons shortening
½ teaspoon soda	1 cup buttermilk
1 teaspoon salt	1 cake yeast or 1 package
3 tablespoons sugar	dry yeast

Warm buttermilk to lukewarm and mix in yeast. Sift dry ingredients together. Cut in shortening. Add milk and yeast mixture. Roll out ¼ inch thick. Cut with a biscuit cutter. Butter tops of each biscuit. Now place one biscuit on top of another to make them ½ inch thick. Let rise until double in size; about one hour. Bake in hot oven (400-425 degrees). When biscuits have cooled, the top and bottom will separate.

Corn Bread Muffins Inez

2 cups plain flour
2 cups cornmeal
4 tablespoons sugar
2 tablespoons baking
  powder

1 teaspoon salt
3 eggs
1 cup milk
1 cup vegetable oil

Heat oven to 425°. In large mixing bowl, mix flour, meal, sugar, baking powder, salt, eggs, milk and oil together. Beat at medium speed until all are mixed well. Grease muffin pan and pour in mixture. Bake for 15 to 20 minutes. Makes 12–16 muffins.

—*Inez Hanna*

Heavenly Hash

1 pint whipping cream
1 bottle maraschino
  cherries
1 box frozen strawberries

½ pound marshmallows
1 can pineapple
1 cup nut meats
1 small bunch grapes

Cut up fruits, nuts, marshmallows. Fold into whipped cream. Place in ice tray and freeze overnight. Serve in squares as dessert or on top of lettuce as salad. Add dressing as desired. Makes 6 servings.

Sweet Potato Casserole

3 cups mashed sweet
  potatoes
1½ cups sugar

2 eggs
1 teaspoon vanilla
½ cup milk

Topping:
⅓ cup margarine
⅔ cup light brown sugar

⅓ cup flour
1 cup chopped nuts

Preheat oven 350 degrees. Mix sweet potatoes, sugar, eggs, vanilla and milk. Pour into buttered casserole dish. Mix topping. Cut margarine into sugar, flour and nuts. Sprinkle over top of casserole. Bake at 350 degrees for 30 minutes.

Banana Pudding

¾ cup sugar
2 tablespoons flour
¼ teaspoon salt
2 cups milk

3 eggs, separated
1 teaspoon vanilla
1 box vanilla wafers
6 bananas

Combine ½ cup sugar, flour, and salt in top of double boiler; stir in milk. Cook over boiling water, stirring constantly, until thickened. Cook uncovered, 15 minutes more. Beat egg yolks, gradually stir in hot mixture. Cook 5 minutes, stirring constantly. Remove from heat, add vanilla.

Line bottom of casserole with vanilla wafers, top with a layer of sliced bananas and wafers.

Beat egg whites, but not dry; gradually add remaining ¼ cup sugar and beat. Bake at 425 for 5 minutes. Serves 6 to 8.

Chicken and Dumplings

The Chicken:

4 lbs. stewing chicken,
    cut up
1½ teaspoon salt
1 medium sized onion,
    cut up

1 carrot, cut
    into pieces
2 ribs celery, cut
    up

Place in Dutch oven, putting the back in first, then giblets, legs and wings, with breast on top. Add boiling water to cover chicken a little more than half; top pieces will steam. Cook. Add vegetables and seasonings. Test for tenderness after 2 hours.

The Dumplings:

2 cups flour
3 tablespoons shortening

1 cup milk

Sift flour, blend in shortening until coarse. Add milk, mix with fork until blended. Drop by tablespoonsful onto chicken pieces. Cook about 25 minutes.

Thin (Lace) Corn Bread Inez

1 cup cornmeal
½ teaspoon salt
4 tablespoons flour

2 tablespoons vegetable
oil
½ cup water

In large mixing bowl, mix meal, salt, flour, oil and water until fully blended. Drop by the tablespoonful like pancakes and fry until golden brown on both sides.

—Inez Hanna

Sweet Potato (Tater) Pie Eddie Mae

½ cup butter
4 medium canned or
   fresh-cooked yams
1 cup sugar
1 teaspoon cinnamon
1 teaspoon nutmeg

½ cup milk
3 eggs
Dash of salt
⅓ cup flour
2 pie shells

Heat oven to 350°. In large mixing bowl, mix potatoes, sugar, cinnamon, salt, eggs and flour. Mix all together until completely mixed. Pour into two pie shells and bake for 45 to 50 minutes or until golden brown.

—Eddie Mae Hall

It should be noted here that years of experience have proven that sweet potato pie is at its best when eaten cold immediately after arriving home from school before going out to play. It is also delicious after play is over and before supper.

Sweet potato pie is such an accepted favorite in Dixie that many rednecks and other culinary experts have almost come to take it for granted. In many homes, a meal without sweet potato pie is like a cheerleader without a pompom.

Finally, no mention of Southern delicacies should be made without including one of the rarest—cracklin' bread.

Crackling bread, commonly referred to as cracklin' bread, is not to be found in just ANY southern restaurant. In fact, most of the spiffy ones in Atlanta have never heard of cracklin' bread, and that's a shame.

For cracklin' bread you have to search out the down-home restaurants that feature home cooking, like Ma Hawkins Restaurant in Dublin, Ga. Not a day goes by that cracklin' bread isn't on the menu, and folks drive many, many miles to eat there because it is.

It is the consensus opinion in middle Georgia that Ma

Hawkins serves up the best cracklin' bread in the south, and has the best team of cooks (not chefs, cooks).

I guess the official name for it, if indeed one is needed, is cracklin' cornbread. And for the benefit of the uneducated, let me hasten to say that a crackling is a piece of pork skin. It comes from a hog and hogs are grown pigs.

Cracklin' bread is really cornbread with little cracklings mixed in, like chocolate chip cookies with chocolate chips mixed in. However, for the benefit of the Yankess, the two (cracklings and chocolate chips) are not inner-changeable.

Here then, and I know you will want to try it, is the recipe for cracklin' bread:

Cracklin' Bread Inez

1½ cups cracklings   4 cups corn meal
4 cups warm water   ½ teaspoon salt

Combine cracklings and water and set aside for 30 minutes. Mix with remaining ingredients. Spoon onto cookie sheet and bake for 30 minutes in a 350° oven.

I NEVER EAT ANYTHING THAT JUMPS, CRAWLS, OR CLIMBS TREES

It is a well-known fact that I am a picky eater. I make no bones about the fact that I don't eat nothin' that bloats, secretes, quivers, shivers, hides in a shell, grins, has whiskers, crawls on the ground or climbs trees. While many of my redneck friends do, I don't. I simply draw the line and stand firm.

My eating habits are legend in middle Georgia.

I was spoiled early in life by one of Georgia's greatest cooks, my mama. She knew what I liked and cooked it. And if there were a Culinary Hall of Fame her roast beef, rice, gravy and biscuits would have made her a charter member. There are nights when I dream about these things.

I have a simple philosophy, and it works well for me: "Don't go nowhere you don't want to go; don't waste time with folks you don't like; and don't eat nothing that don't appeal to you."

The last thing new I tried was Hamburger Helper. I liked it, and I think it ought to be on restaurant menus.

Here are some of the things I don't eat:

• I don't eat snails for the simple reason that I ain't eatin' nothin' that looks like Don Knotts and can't outrun Jackie Gleason.

• I don't eat chicken livers or gizzards. I'll leave them for the pathologists. Plus, I ain't never figured out what a gizzard is, or does.

• I don't eat frog legs because I ain't gonna' challenge nothin' that can stand flat-footed and jump higher than me.

• I don't eat casseroles due to the fact that I ain't puttin' nothin' in my mouth that I can't identify. Plus, the things look like after-thoughts, yesterday's leftovers.

- I don't eat deer meat (venison) because when I see it I think of Bambi.
- I don't eat Italian or Chinese food because I balk at devouring anything I can't pronounce.
- I don't eat doves because I don't eat dark meat. Quail, yes. Doves and ducks, no.
- I don't eat hot fried chicken. Heck, I don't even eat warm fried chicken. The waitresses and cooks where I eat most of my meals automatically see to it that my fried chicken goes in the freezer for at least 10 minutes before serving.
- I don't eat Chinese food. I've already told you that. But I do go to Chinese restaurants with friends who do. I simply order rice because I don't eat nothin' that looks like it ain't through growin'.
- I don't eat egg drop soup. I might try it if it had a different name.
- I don't eat eggplant. By any other name it might be palatable. But like egg drop soup, I automatically pass it up.
- I do eat ice cream, but only vanilla. I don't play musical churns when it comes to ice cream.
- I don't eat cottage cheese because it has no taste. Cottage cheese is for the sick and elderly.
- I don't eat squash. It sounds like it has already been eaten. Change the name, and I might try it.
- I don't eat squid. I ain't about to eat nothin' that will attack a submarine.
- I don't eat beets. They appear to have been in a bad wreck, and suffered multiple bruises.
- I don't eat boiled cabbage because I have no desire to still taste on Thursday morning what I ate Monday night. The same goes for cucumbers.
- I don't partake of iced coffee or hot tea. I just don't think the good Lord intended them to be served that way.
- I don't eat pig brains and eggs. Ugh! Forget it! I got caught in the middle of that mess a few years back, and I still haven't fully recovered.
- I don't eat from buffets. I think this stems primarily from the fact that I've never learned to manipulate a salad bowl, a plate, silverware, a cup and saucer, a napkin and a dessert dish all at the same time without

dropping something. Also, buffets always feature deformed chickens, all backs and wings.

So, what pray tell do I like to eat? Easy.

If I should have to choose a final meal, I wouldn't hesitate for a New York minute (somewhat faster than your ordinary minute). I'd order barbequed ribs. I often lust after barbequed ribs. I have driven 300 miles (to Atlanta and back) just to satisfy my urge for barbequed ribs.

The best barbequed ribs in the south are served in Atlanta (Skeeter's); in Savannah (Johnny Harris'); and Nashville (Tony Roma's). And to give credit where credit is due, there are two places north of the Mason–Dixon line that are blue ribbon barbequed rib eating establishments: Russel's Steak House in Detroit, and Don Stampler's Steak Joint (Greenwich Village) in New York.

You have probably noticed that no mention has been

made of oysters. I will do so now, and you can take this to the bank: I am convinced that the bravest man who ever lived was the first man to eat an oyster. (And the hungriest.)

And now, a final word about collards, a traditional Southern delicacy. Collards are always plural. You just can't beg, borrow or steal one collard.

I've always considered collards to be out of place down in Dixie. They should be an eastern dish, up in New Jersey or New York where people eat funny things like pumpernickel bread and yogurt. I'd rather take a dose of castor oil than eat collards.

SECTION THREE

LIFESTYLES BELOW
THE GNAT LINE

THE GNAT LINE

The gnat line is peculiar to my home state of Georgia. It is accepted as fact that the gnat line is synonomous with the fall line, that being a line that follows an area commonly known as the Sand Hills of Georgia. The line extends from Augusta on the east to Columbus on the west, traveling through Macon. It is the dividing line between the Southern Piedmont Plain and the South Central Plain. It is in the area of the fall (or gnat) line that the terrain levels off between the hills and mountains of North Georgia and the flat and sandy South Georgia country.

The gnat is a necessary evil in South Georgia. They annoy many animals, including man, and are so small that they can pass through window screening. They come with the territory.

Georgia natives learn early in life to cope with gnats by simply blowing them away from their mouth and eyes, while northerners frantically wave at them with their hands.

Technically speaking, the gnats found in Georgia are Eye gnats and belong to the genus Hippelates of the family Chloropidae, but I doubt seriously that the gnats themselves know that. They do, however, know where the gnat line is and abide by it because few are found north of it. But billions make their summer home south of it.

The gnat is an uninvited and unwelcomed guest at such places as picnics, barbeques, fish fries, church dinners on the grounds, or any other outdoor activity where food is served.

There are those in gnat country, however, who feel that the little pest has redeeming value as demonstrated by this wording on an often-seen T-shirt in gnat country: "Preserve The Gnat; Otherwise We'll Be Up To Our Necks In Yankees!"

A REDNECK'S DOUBLE-WIDE IS HIS CASTLE

There's a great story still making the rounds in South Georgia concerning the separation and ultimate divorce of one Buster and his wife, Johnny Faye.

Buster and Johnny Faye had been in a state of disagreement for weeks, she accusing him of being unfaithful while he rebutted with the fact that she was not a good mother. The continuing argument peaked on a Saturday night after they had attended the weekly dance at the VFW Club in a nearby town.

"Well, I'll just tell you this!" Buster shouted as he drove to their trailer from the dance. "I have a good mind to just tell ever'body we know that I went to bed with you 'fore we ever got married! Now then, whatta' you think o' that?"

Johnny Faye bristled, and came back with, "Oh, yeah? Well, you jus' go right ahead and do that. Know what I'll do?"

"Whut?" grumbled Buster.

"I'll jus' go right behin' you and tell 'em that you won't the onliest one!"

Naturally, the divorce was forthcoming. It was finalized thirty days later and one night Buster was talking about the property settlement while shooting eight-ball in Hawkeye's Pool Room, a regular haunt for him and one of the prime factors contributing to his and Johnny Faye's divorce.

"Ever'thing went smooth as silk," he said between shots. "We jus' split ever'thing 50–50—including the double-wide."

A glance of suspicion and disbelief was cast by Hawkeye, who asked, "Aw, c'mon, Buster. How'n th' hell can you split a trailer 50–50?"

"Plumb easy, man," said Buster as he banked the

nine-ball in the side pocket and chalked up to zero in on the eight. "She got th' inside an' I got th' outside."

And . . . he missed the eight-ball, straight in the corner pocket. A rarity for Buster.

It really isn't hard to spot a redneck house or trailer. Certain characteristics sort of jump out at you.

Let's take a look at the outside first.

You will find most rednecks to be three-car families; one in the front yard, usually of about 1968 vintage, with all four wheels off and sitting on four cement blocks; one in the back yard with the motor out and sitting on the ground, usually a '72 Chevrolet Impala; and the third, a '76 pickup in limited running condition, parked in front of the house under a shade tree. A dog, also in limited running condition, will be stretched out under the pickup.

In the back of the truck will be a number of crushed beer cans, a gasoline can, a five-foot section of a water hose for siphoning purposes, a coiled chain of undetermined length for towing, a dog box, a tool chest, a fishing tackle box, two fishing rods and two reels (one that works and one that don't), three blocks of wood of undetermined origin, three cans of oil and two empty oil cans, five spent shotgun shells, a spare tire (flat), a jack and three used pistons, and a boat paddle.

Inside the cab, on the dash, are three or four boxes of matches, two empty Winston cigarette packages, a beer opener, several pieces of string, sixty-seven cents in assorted coins, a State Farm Insurance calendar (opened to November although it's April), roughly 27 envelopes representing three month's overdue bills, three bolts and two nuts that fit nothing, a knife with a broken blade, a screwdriver with a broken handle, two empty boiled peanut bags, a four-year-old W-2 form, a Spearmint chewing gum wrapper, two Skoal snuff cans (one empty and the other half-filled), a throwaway letter from his congressman and a broken comb.

On the seat are two-year-old copies of *Playboy* and *Penthouse*, along with a current issue of *Parts Pups*, several cassette tapes by favorite country music artists, a publicity photograph of Dolly Parton, two cans of Vienna sausage, half a box of saltines and a Hershey bar. Also, a deck of cards, a pair of dice, two fishing lures, a small box of fish hooks, half a box of .12 gauge shotgun shells, a fish stringer, an empty Jack Daniels bottle, two Beef Jerkys, a Harold Robbins paperback and three hair curlers.

On the floorboard on the passenger side is a dirty T-shirt, one sneaker, three socks, two McDonald's Egg McMuffin cartons, a Hardee's coffee cup, two empty paper sacks, a pair of pliers, a crowbar, several receipts from K-Mart, two empty Levi Garrett packs, many tabs from pop-top beer cans, an equal number of Winston cigarette butts, two pieces of cuestick chalk and a county tax notice (unpaid).

Hanging in the rear window are a 30.06 deer rifle, a .12 gauge Remington Model 1100 automatic shotgun and a personalized cuestick. Also a window sticker that reads, "Member NRA."

On the back bumper are these bumper stickers: "American By Birth And Southern By The Grace Of God," "If You Must Criticize The Farmers, Don't Talk With Your Mouth Full," "Hell No, I Ain't Forgettin'!"

On the front bumper, these: "Get Your Heart In America Or Get Your Ass Out," "Southern Born And Southern Bred, And When I Die I'll Be Southern Dead," "I Found It." And a personalized plate that reads, "Joe Boy and Willie Kate."

So much for the pickup. A quick look around the yard and you'll see these trademarks:

- A tire swing hanging from a tree.
- Three or four young 'uns hanging from a tree.
- A broken TV antenna.
- A satellite dish that works.
- A washer and dryer on the front porch.
- Several chickens and a cat or two on the steps and porch.
- 12 syrup cans containing geraniums lining the walk to the front porch.
- Half-buried king-size Coke bottles between the syrup cans, just for effect.
- Half-buried white-washed automobile tires lining the driveway. Some rotted, others needing more whitewash.
- The remains of a picket fence out by the road.
- Two bicycle tires in what was once a flower bed.
- Two mud puddles, one in the front yard and one in the back.
- A worn and rusty Honda 125 and an equally worn and rusty go-cart propped up next to the tree holding the tire swing.
- One set of bedsprings behind the utility shed.
- Another set of bed-springs in front of the utility shed.
- Three fishing poles leaning against the utility shed.
- A small pile of used bricks under the front steps.
- Three 55-gallon drums in the vicinity of the back door.
- One partially-finished barbeque cooker, made from a 55-gallon drum.
- One inflatable swimming pool, long ago deflated and now filled with pine needles and tadpoles. Plus a shoe and two baby diapers.

REDNECKS CAN BE A LITTLE SENSITIVE ABOUT YANKEE INSULTS

My friend Robbie Nell Bell is the head waitress and music lover in charge of the jukebox at Mel's Juke and Bobby-Q about a six-pack north of Braxton. She's as real as streak-o-lean, salt mackerel, and chitlins. She lives for country music, Salem Light 100s, Budweiser, and "my two young'uns, who live with my mommer."

At Mel's Juke and Bobby-Q she feeds quarters to the jukebox like a trained seal handler hands out dead fish. Just over a year ago she came face to face with a pair of New Jersey Americans in Mel's. We all can learn from how she handled the encounter.

The female of the pair sported a wrinkled suntan that all her friends at the deli in Jersey City would drool over.

The guy wore shorts and sandals and puffed on a big black cigar as long as a hoe handle that smelled like George Blackshear's cow lot on a rainy morning.

They selected a booth next to the very operative jukebox and the broken coat rack.

Robbie Nail closed in, leaned on the counter, and asked, "Y'all want bobby-q?"

"Do we have a choice?" asked the female New Jersey American.

"I reckon so. We got slyce't an' cheeupped."

"Is that all you'se got?" asked the male.

"Nope. We got pickled pigs feet and Slim Jims," she answered.

"Uggghh," grunted the female.

"Bring us two chipped with plenty of hot sauce," demanded the male.

"Anythin' to drink? We got Coke an' beer."

The male chose beer; the disappointed female selected

Coke after determining there was no Tab.

In due time, after two heartbreaking selections on the jukebox, "I'm a Warm Hearted Man but Mama's Got Cold Feet" and "When Your Girlfriend Writes a Letter to Your Wife," Robbie Nail slid the bobby-q sandwiches, cheeupped, and the drinks in front of the furriners.

Within seconds, the male voiced another demand.

"Hey, girl! I specifically asked for hot sauce. Up where we come from people know how to season food. Don't you have any hot bar-becue sauce? This stuff is awful," he ranted.

She motioned for Mel to join her in the back.

"Ya' got any of Y'r Aunt Minnie's hot pepper sauce left fum Christmas, Mel? Them Yankees out there in the front booth don't like y'r bobby-q sauce. The man says it ain't hot enough."

"Hmmmmm, lemme see. Last time I saw it I used it to start my outboard motor. It was right here by the kerosene and . . . oh yeah, here 'tis. But be careful," Mel cautioned.

After a generous dousing

of both sandwiches with Aunt Minnie's special hot pepper sauce, Robbie Nail again slid them in front of the New Jersey Americans—and waited. But she didn't have to wait long.

"There, that's more like it," mumbled the male as he chomped on a large bite of his cheeupped and loaded bobby-q sandwich. You just have to show these people down here in the South how to . . . Aaaahhh! Wheeewww! I'm on fiirrrre! Great God Almighty, my mouth is on fiirre! Water! Water! Bring me water, quick!"

Robbie Nail and Mel watched as he did an Indian fire dance past the juke, over a tackle box, and out the front door. His wife followed suit with her version of a New Jersey belly dancer before running into Hawkeye's Jeep.

When last seen, both were in the big ol' Cadillac, eating grapefruit and oranges by the dozen, and trying to get the car started.

"Yankee go home!" yelled Robbie Nail.

"And stay there!" echoed Mel.

Robbie Nail dropped a quarter in the juke, the cheeupped bobby-q sandwiches in the garbage can, and mumbled, "Mel, I jus' plain don't like no Yankees comin' down here an' tellin' me 'bout how t' fix bobby-q."

"Me neither, Robbie Nail. Now, how 'bout wipin' up that hot pepper sauce before it eats a hole in the counter," Mel said.

THE CELEBRATION

I was in Willacoochee for the third annual Old Fashion Day Celebration complete with boiled peanuts, homemade cakes and cookies, gospel music, political speeches and handshaking. And there was also a guided tour, buses furnished, where a stranger could see the likes of McCranie's liquor still (no mention in the official program as to the whereabouts of McCranie), an obsolete Chevrolet (I could have shown 'em an obsolete Mercury) and obsolete Ford parts.

This special notation appeared on the printed program:

"Bus Available For A Tour of McCranie's Still Every Hour Beginning At 10:00." (But it didn't indicate a.m. or p.m.)

Of course, Willacoochee's main attraction, The No Name Bar, the town's only shrine, made famous by the typewriter of Lewis Grizzard, wasn't mentioned.

I arrived in town shortly after noon. My first stop was at a dedication ceremony where a T-33 airplane that crashed in Willacoochee while on a training mission was being unveiled.

A local good ol' boy who made it big in the Air Force, and is now the commanding general at Warner Robins, handled the speechmaking. He was assisted by Mayor Futch and other various and sundry politicians.

I left the airplane dedication and drove through downtown Willacoochee enroute to the main event, the arts and crafts show.

I'll tell you, friends, Willachoochee was jumping and moving. I'll wager there hasn't been that much action in town since the morning after a pair of good ol' boys broke into the local drug store a few years back and stole all the Ex-Lax "candy."

When I arrived at the arts and crafts show, nestled in a bunch of Atkinson County pines, peanuts were boiling, babies were crying, politicians were shaking hands and gospel groups were singing. The women sat in folding chairs under a funeral home tent and fanned gnats with funeral home fans while the men stood around, chewed tobacco, shook hands and promised to vote for every politician in sight.

One old gentleman blew it when asked by a candidate for his vote.

"Well, I'll think about it if'n I can manage enough extra cash to pay my poll tax."

Like I said, it was Old Fashion Day in Willacoochee . . . real old.

I bought some boiled peanuts and a Coke before taking a seat under the tent to listen to "The Gospel Boys," from Douglas. They were getting it on with "Bound For the Glory Land," and the lady seated next to me was keeping time with her funeral home fan. I offered her some boiled peanuts.

"No, thank ya'. I done ate two bags. Them ol' Gospel Boys is all right, ain't they?"

she said.

"Yes ma'am. They're real good," I agreed.

"I jus' come back from Florida, m'sef. My baby boy lives down there. He plays and sings, too. An' I tell ya' one thing—he can flat tear a pea-anner up," she allowed.

"Yessum, I bet he can," I said. (When a mama says her baby boy can "flat tear a pea-anner up," I'm gonna' go along with it.)

I got up shortly and began to circulate among the crowd but stopped when I just happened to notice this girl sauntering by. She had the posture of a ruptured ostrich and sported a pair of shorts cut down below her navel. You know, the kind you see every Saturday morning at the mall.

The girl was puffing on a cigarette and drinking "something" from a paper cup. She stopped walking long enough to exchange pleasantries with an obvious acquaintance.

"Hey, Judy! Whatcha' doin', ya' lazy heifer?" she yelled.

"Oh, nothin' in p'ticklar. Jus' waitin f'r Roy," Judy replied. "Where ya' headed?"

"Jus' cruisin'. Goin' to th' dance t'nite? I hear tell Half-Pint and The Country Boys is playin'."

"Dang right! I'll be there if Roy's truck'll run."

I left the arts and crafts following a good speech by Joe Frank Harris and, out of allegiance to my friend, Lewis Grizzard, stopped in at The No Name Bar where the bartenders were changing shifts, Clayton going off and Bill coming on.

It's no wonder the locals call the place "The Shrine of St. Lewis." The guy's picture and newspaper columns are all over the walls.

Bill allowed as how Grizzard is a good fella', and I didn't argue with that.

"I guess ol' Lewis has really put this place on the map, huh?" I commented.

"Yep, he's done that. Business is real good. But th' boy causes problems now and again."

"What do you mean, problems?" I asked.

"Well, ever' time he writes one o' them dang colyums 'bout th' joint we have so much business a fella' can't hardly git off t' go fishin' er' nothin'," Bill said.

"Hmmmm, I see what you mean. And a fella' don't need to ever let business get in the way of his fishin' or nothin'," I replied.

"Dang right!" Bill agreed.

I stayed at The No Name just long enough to listen to an argument after a customer spit on the floor. And that, friend, is a no-no at The No Name.

"Just ain't right, fella' spittin' on th' floor. An' he won't even chewin'," Bill philosphized. "I do a lot of things what ain't right but I don't spit on no man's floor."

"Me neither," echoed a customer seated at the bar. "Hell, I'm 46 years old but my daddy'd tear my tail up if I done that."

"Well, he ort to," Bill said.

And that's the way it goes day in and day out at the bar in Willacoochee, the town's only shrine, immortalized by Lewis Grizzard.

I left shortly, but not before kneeling, saying three "Hail Lewises," and dropping $2.40 in the collection plate.

Spit on the floor? You couldn't pay me enough to do that at The No Name. That'd get me in more trouble than calling the patron saint of The No Name Bar a Yankee.

I only have one regret concerning my journey to Willacoochee. I'd love to have heard that lady's baby boy "just flat tear up a pea-anner."

POLITICS

One wag is reported to have said that in the south politics is everything. Anyone who watches the game being played knows it's everything for the politicians, for sure. And it's everything for the people who depend on the business that political connections bring them. But the ordinary citizen looks upon all the hoopla with a combination of humor and cynicism.

Personally, I like election years. They're a lot like New Year's Eve. You know, resolutions, party platforms, warranties and whatever. I always liked it when, for years, perennial candidate for governor "Fat" Baker outlined his campaign. "I'm only running for one reason—to prove that an honest man can't win." (He never won. You can draw your own conclusions.)

And there was Eugene Talmadge's famous put-down of a heckler during one of his speeches on a hot July day in deep south Georgia.

"Tell us 'bout all that money you stole, Gene!" yelled the heckler.

"I stole it! I stole every nickel of it" bellowed Talmadge to the huge crowd, mostly farmers. "But I stole it for you boys out there in overalls!"

The story goes on that the heckler barely escaped with his life.

And there was the time when Harry Truman was reportedly interrupted during one of his whistle-stop speeches in 1948 with, "Tell us all you know, Harry! It won't take but a few seconds."

"I'll just tell you all we both know, friend. It won't take a damn bit longer," Truman shot back.

Here in Georgia, it is standard procedure in an election year to throw barbeques and fish fries for the candidates. Naturally, these bring out the political freeloaders. Like Gus Groover and Luke Jordan over in Emanuel County, for instance.

Gus and Luke haven't bought a Friday or Saturday night supper in an election year since Franklin D. Roosevelt's first term. And they're selective, too.

"You goin' to Harry Holtzclough's fish fry tonight, Gus?"

"Don't think so, Luke. Goin' to the one at Collins' camphouse for Wilbur Crimmins. I just like trout better'n mullet. Besides, Lucy Gordon makes better hushpuppies than Martha Mincey does. Martha don't put in enough onion," replied Gus.

"Well, you're right 'bout that. How 'bout the barbeque at the river for Jack Butterworth tomorrow night? Goin'?" Luke asked.

"Naw, I'm goin to Slick Criswell's shrimp supper. Went to Jack's last election, and as I remember they weren't no beer. I saw Buster Lumley at the courthouse this mornin' and he told me Slick ordered 25 cases of Miller," Gus said.

"Dern! I'm with you on that, Gus."

The story goes that shortly after Marvin Griffin's victory for the governorship in 1958, Gus and Luke freeloaded on up to Atlanta to attend the victory celebration, a gala affair held in the Henry Grady ballroom. Gus even bought new overalls and Luke got a haircut.

After finishing a main course of what Luke called "some kind of bird" a waiter inquired of him if he'd like dessert.

"Yeah, sounds good. Bring me some," he said.

"What would you like, sir?"

"Pie. Bring me a piece of pie,"

"What kind, sir?"

"What kind?" Luke bellowed. "Tater pie, boy, what the hell do you think pie's made out of?"

A REUNION OF SORTS

I just happened to see Luke and Gus at a basketball game a couple of weeks ago. I presumed both would be anxiously awaiting the next election year.

"How y'all doin'?" I asked.

"Fine, doin' fine," Gus said.

"Can't complain," said Luke. "How 'bout y'sef?"

"Everything's hunkydorey," I said.

I hadn't seen either in over 20 years. They hadn't changed much.

"All set for those fish fries and barbeques? Election year's coming up you know?"

"Yeah. We'll be right there at ever one of 'em," said Gus.

"Wouldn't miss one if I had the measles," Luke said.

"Made up your mind as to who you'll vote for in the governor's race yet?" I asked.

"Not me," said Luke. "I ain't voted since they put them votin' machines in 'bout 10 years ago."

"Why not, Luke?"

"Ain't hardly worth the bother to come to town and just vote once. Can't vote but one time on them machines, you know," he sighed.

"What about you, Gus?"

"Who, me? Shoot, I don't vote," he snickered.

"Why not?"

"Ain't never registered."

RELIGION SHOWS UP IN THE MOST AMAZING PLACES

I really hadn't planned to have dinner at Jo-Jo's Gulf and House of Prayer. My original plan was to have it at the Nic-Nac Dining Room in Statesboro, one of Georgia's most underrated eating establishments.

But when you head out in a 17-year-old Mercury to visit your 22-year-old daughter you just eat wherever the car conks out. Last Sunday it happened to be Jo-Jo's Gulf and House of Prayer somewhere between Swainsboro and Portal.

The sign in front fascinated me as I guided my Mercury with the ruptured radiator off Highway 80.

> **"Jo-Jo's Gulf Service Station and House of Prayer JESUS IS COMING SOON! Cold Beer To Go"**

"Are you Jo-Jo?" I asked the man who came out of the station.

"Well, I'm one of 'em," he replied. "Other one's in prayer meetin'."

I played it straight. I mean, you don't get cute when you're treading on Jo-Jo's turf and he has inside information about the Second Coming of Christ. Cold beer to go? I didn't dare pursue that. And there was singing in the back, behind the grease rack.

"Looks like I've got radiator problems. Can you help me out?" I asked.

He looked at me like I was speaking Russian. Then, he checked his pocket watch. That was a clue. I trust any man who carries a pocket watch.

"I'll see what I can do as soon as prayer meetin's over. Be 'bout 45 minutes I reckon." he told me.

"Fine, I'll wait. I'll just eat a bite while I'm waiting," I said.

"That's alright by me. Just

set over there by the cash register and if anybody comes up tell 'em to come back after prayer meeting'," he said. "Dog's name is Punjab. He don't bite."

"Thanks, neither do I," I said trying to make a joke. After all, you have to take a chance now and then.

Joe made no reply. Neither did Punjab. In fact, he never moved a muscle until I opened a can of tuna and a package of saltines.

We finished off the tuna and crackers and I couldn't help but notice that Punjab isn't nearly as pretty as my daughter. Their appetites are similar but their faces are different.

Punjab went back to his corner to dream about whatever bulldogs dream about

and I gave some thought to all the other times and places I've had a car conk out.

"I've had 'em go out in Texas, Michigan, New York, California. You name it. Savannah? Many times. New Jersey? Once is enough.

Just once I'd like for my car to conk out in Savannah within walking distance of Williams Seafood Restaurant or The Pirate's House. No such luck. Know where it happens? Right in front of Shag's Hamburgers and Pool Room, and the chalk is tastier than the hamburgers.

In Texas my usual run of luck was to conk out somewhere in tumbleweed country between Alice and Falfurias and roll to a stop near Rosa's Tortilla House. I

think every Mexican who ever scooted across the Rio Grande at one time or another opened a tortilla house.

Have you ever eaten a tortilla? Cardboard ala carte is tastier.

There must be hundreds of excellent restaurants in New Jersey. You'd think the odds would let me conk out in front of one, huh? No way.

I'd limp to a stop in front of Dominick's Pizza and Numbers House. Heck, I wouldn't eat pizza in Rome let alone in Rahway, New Jersey.

Once, in San Francisco, my brakes failed and I zoomed right on by The Fisherman's Wharf and I finally stopped at some joint called "Lula's Place • Home Cooking • If Lula Ain't Got It, You Can't Get It."

One look at Lula's apron and I ordered hard-boiled eggs. She obviously hadn't changed or washed it since World War II. But it was an expensive apron. It had to be, it had at least $27 worth of mustard, catsup and eggs on it. Punjab wouldn't have eaten at Lula's.

Lula's Place burned to the ground a few years ago, prompting one regular to comment, "Well, that's the first time the food's been hot in Lula's since she opened up."

NEW RADIATOR HOSE, FRIED CHICKEN AND HIT THE ROAD

My concentration was broken when Jo entered, accompanied by a woman carrying a Bible under her arm.

"This here's my wife, Jo. You eat?" he asked.

"Right, I had a can of tuna and some crackers. The money's on the register," I told him.

Punjab had heard enough. He rolled over, stretched and went back to sleep.

"Well, lemme' see 'bout that radiator," he said. "Jo, why don't you get this fella' a couple of pieces of chicken left over from dinner; and a couple of biscuits."

In an hour I had a new radiator hose, a belly full of fried chicken and biscuits and I was on my way. I had something else, too. Two new friends. Well, three if you count Punjab.

And the chicken was delicious. Lula would have loved it.

One thing I learned at Jo-Jo's Gulf Station and House of Prayer; all breakdowns aren't for the worst.

SMALL TOWN AMERICA

The key to understanding Dixie is realizing that at heart it is small town America. Makes no difference about the number of people who live there. The small town is as much a matter of the heart as it is size.

But since small towns are where most people go first when looking for rednecks, I've included some information on how you know you're in one.

You know you're in a small town when:

• The airport runway is terraced.

• Square dancing is more popular than disco on Saturday night.

• Third Street is out on the edge of town.

• Every sport is played on dirt.

• The editor and publisher (one and the same) of the town weekly carries a camera at all times.

• You don't use turn signals because everybody knows where you're going.

• Your baby is born June 13 and you receive gifts from the local merchants because it's the first baby of the year.

• You speak to each dog you pass by name, and he wags his tail at you.

• You dial a wrong number and talk for 15 minutes anyway.

• You are run off Main Street by a combine.

• You can't walk for exercise because every car that passes offers you a ride.

• The local paper devotes half of the front page to your wedding.

• You run your car into a ditch five miles out of town and the word gets back before you do.

• You write a check on the wrong bank and it covers for you.

• You miss church one Sunday and receive a get

well card on Tuesday.

• Someone asks how you feel and listens to what you say because they really want to know.

• The biggest business in town sells machinery.

HERE ARE A FEW MORE

You also know you're in a small town when:

• The head of the Mafia is a little Japanese guy.

• The local truck stop is a nail.

• The biggest church in town is the Fourth Baptist.

• The Rotary Club meeting is cancelled because the guy can't get off work at lunch time.

• The train stops in town and the engine is out in the country.

• City Hall has hump-backed mice.

• The grocer hands you your change from a $5 bill and you don't bother to count it.

• When both city limit signs are on the same post.

• Most of the houses have front porches.

• The doctor makes house calls.

• Downtown is as quiet on Thursday afternoon as the local cemetery.

• There is no line at the local cafe after Sunday morning church services.

• You help your neighbor paint his house—and he helps you paint yours.

• Marijuana is some little town down in Mexico.

• "Coke" is a soft drink that burns your nose when, after drinking it, you burp.

• You only hear "go-go" from the town stutterer.

• The emptiest building in town is the City Jail.

• Everybody loves the policeman, the school principal and the barber.

• There are more people standing on the sidewalk in front of the stores talking, than there are inside shopping.

• All stores have counter checks and no identification is required to cash one.

• There are more pickups than cars on the street.

• The county fair is the social event of the year.

• Gospel records outsell hard rock 10 to 1.

• "Pot" is still that little item that sits under the edge of the bed.

Thank God for small towns and the people who live in them. They are the backbone of America.

SECTION FOUR

THE FINER POINTS OF SOUTHERN LIFE

WORDS YOU HEAR IN THE SOUTH

I was enjoying a hot dog and a Coke in the Dublin Mall last Saturday when I heard the lady seated at the next table say it.

"Well, she's alright, just a little 'uppity,' that's all."

That's what the lady said and the word that caught my attention was "uppity." It's a dang good word and the only one that fits to characterize some people.

I really don't know why but when referring to the ladies the word employed is usually "uppity," but the same reference to a man prompts the use of another catch-word, "biggety."

I remember my younger days back in Oglethorpe and ol' Bully Barfield. Bully was "biggety." He drove a Packard convertible, went to Macon whenever he took a notion and always parked in front of the courthouse on Saturday afternoon so everybody could see him drinking RCs and eatin' boiled peanuts, 'specially Buttercup Hill who drove a '34 Ford and raised them peanuts ol' Bully was eatin'.

"Bully's biggety," Buttercup used to say. "The biggety____ain't hit a lick since his daddy died an' left him that car."

The more I considered the words *uppity* and *biggety* last Saturday, the more I reflected on other words and phrases that supplemented the vocabularies of some adults back in my boyhood days.

Take Mrs. Allen, in Oglethorpe, for instance. I can almost hear her words now as I recall her discussions with her preacher regarding the song service in her church.

"Well, preacher, you got Ralph Blackford up there leadin' the singin' an' he don't know 'diddley' 'bout music," she'd say.

"Diddley?" Ralph don't know "diddley?" I attempted to look it up in my un-abridged dictionary. No luck.

Question: If Ralph "don't know diddley 'bout music" just exactly what and how much doesn't Ralph know 'bout music"? (Of course, I'm not even sure the word *diddley* is spelled "d-i-d-d-l-e-y.")

Another favorite, and one I've heard all my life but still have no earthly idea what one is, is "hissie." What the heck is a "hissie?"

I can't count on my fingers and toes the number of times I've heard some adult say, "Boy, if your Daddy saw you doin' that he'd have a hissie fit."

Dictionary? I tried it. No "hissie (hissy)" to be found.

I've seen people pitch his-sie fits. In fact, at the ripe old age of five, I pitched one at my grandmother's house up in Hancock County on a Sunday morning. You proba-bly ain't gonna' believe this, but here is the reason I pitched it.

I wanted to wear a bra to church. O.K., I'll repeat it. I wanted to wear a bra to church. Know what? The hissie fit worked because I wore that booger to the Powelton Methodist Church, sat there strapped as big as life and sang with my mother, grandmother and four aunts, although admit-tedly "I didn't know diddley 'bout music."

Then, there is another type fit that has been with us a long time. Somehow, I get the feeling that it's milder and much less demonstrative than a "hissie fit."

Of course, I'm referring to

the "conniption fit," undoubtedly a more dignified fit than the "hissie" because it's listed in my dictionary.

So, if you're determined to pitch a fit, may I suggest the conniption variety? Then, at least the person for whose benefit you're pitching it can look it up in the dictionary and know what you're doing. I mean, why pitch a fit if nobody knows what it is you're doing, right?

Let us continue with this nonsense. Grandpa had his favorite expressions like when he'd tell some of his checkerplaying chums in his old country store about his bulldog, Scrappy.

I never once heard Grandpa say Scrappy could run fast, that he was a speedster or "can run like a scared deer." Nope. None of these. But I heard him say many times over that ol' Scrappy could go "lickety-split."

Lickety-split? Right. And it's in the dictionary, too, right under what Mama used to give me just before sending me off to a birthday party at Carolyn LeGrande's house in Lumpkin, a "lick-and-a-promise."

I remember Mr. Dan Kleckley, who owned a grocery store where the men gathered every morning, sat on benches out front, opened their mail and told hunting and fishing lies.

Mr. Dan gave the same reply every morning when greeted by his visitors with, "How're you feelin' this mornin', Dan?"

"Fair to middlin'," he'd say.

I know this. "Fair-to-middlin'" must be pretty good because Mr. Dan lived to a ripe old age.

SAYIN' IT SOUTHERN

Certainly all regions of America have their own particular expressions that are identifiable with a certain area and its people. They are handed down from generation to generation, and here are some peculiar to the South, rednecks and country gentlemen alike.

"He's too lazy to hit a lick at a snake."

"This knife's so dull it wouldn't cut hot butter."

"It's cold as a well-digger's tail."

"He's just as happy as if he had good sense."

"That boy can run faster than greased lightning."

"It was rough as a cob."

"This here's better'n snuff, an' ain't half as dusty."

"She's pretty as a speckled puppy."

"I'm full as a tick."

"That ol' boy's tough as whit leather."

"She's fat as a tub o' lard."

"She's limber as a dishrag."

"He ran like a scalded dog."

"She was as nervous as a long-tailed cat in a room full of rocking chairs."

"She's so ugly she'd run a dog off'n a meat wagon."

"He took off like Moody's goose."

"That stuff's as scarce as hen's teeth."

"Now, don't go gittin' y'r feathers ruffled."

"She's flat as a pancake."

"The creek's dry as a bone."

"I'm sober as a judge."

"He's wild as a buck."

"I'm stiff as a board."

"It's right as rain."

"I picked him clean as a whistle."

"He's crazy as a bedbug."

"That's 'bout as funny as a crutch."

"I'm mad as fire."

"He's wet as a drowned rat."

"He's dead as a doornail."

"He was steppin' in high cotton."

"I'm eatin' high off'n the hog."

"Looks to me like he's playin' possum."

"I really gave her a piece of my mind."

"I'm doin' tolerable well."

"The family's all in table order" (able to come to the table and eat).

"She was as surprised as a June bride."

"Don't y'all act up, you heah?"

"He ain't no 'count, nohow."

"If'n it ain't right, I'm gonna' raise sand."

"He's wild as a peach orchard hog."

"He's so poor he'd have to borrow money to buy water to cry with."

"I'd do it in a New York minute."

"He's so buck-toothed he could eat corn-on-the-cob through a keyhole."

"It's soft as a baby's butt."

"He's slick as an eel."

"He's happy as a kid with a new toy."

"He took off like a striped ape."

"She's sorry as a two-dollar watch."

"He's th' spittin' image o' his daddy."

"That party was a stem-winder."

"I tell ya', I'm plumb tuckered out."

"He flat throwed a hissie fit."

"He's got more money than th' law allows."

"She's got more cousins than Carter's got liver pills."

"He's tough as a lightered knot."

"She's proud as a baby in a new buggy."

"That ol' boy was up the creek without a paddle."

"He's got more freckles than a dog's got fleas."

"He's done gone an' got Yankee rich."

"Ya' better bleeve it!"

"You got that right."

STORY TELLIN'

Southerners—including rednecks—are the happiest when they're telling stories. I've included the following stories because I believe they say more about what it means to be a true Southerner than anything I could write.

◆ ◆ ◆ ◆ ◆

Ol' Toby amassed a fortune in the moonshine business. Since he was a jug supplier on the side, I guess you could call him a double-dipper.

Toby lived in a modest home, a two-bedroom job, in a modest neighborhood dotted by jacked-up '58 Plymouths, orphaned transmissions from vintage '62 junkers, and hubcaps of every description, some too hot to pick up. But Toby wanted more; he wanted status, and indoor plumbing. He didn't have the respect he felt a good, hard-working bootlegger deserved. He wanted to move to the doctor and lawyer neighborhood. And he did.

Much to the chagrin of the GP's, surgeons and barristers, Toby the Bootlegger bought a home priced in the general range of the federal deficit. He moved in and set up housekeeping, proud to have bought a little status. But, he had a shock in store. He soon learned that his was the only house in the neighborhood without a swimming pool, and all his neighbors were diving and splashing late at night in theirs. Plus, the going thing was to go "skinny-dipping" at midnight in your own pool.

Toby vowed that when he made his next "run" he would take care of the pool situation. He did, and had an Olympic-size job installed in his back yard. He could hardly wait for the pool to fill and fantasized about his first midnight swim, sans bathing suit.

It was a steaming August night when Toby stripped down in his bedroom over-looking his new swimming pool. Toby would momen-tarily join his neighbors for the traditional midnight swim.

Toby raised the bedroom window and sailed in, splashing water 30 feet high. (Let us remember that Toby weighed in at a nifty 365). But, there was an immediate problem. Toby never took the time off from his bootlegging activities to learn to swim, and there he was gurgling and strangling in the deep end of his Olympic prize.

A doctor-neighbor, a respi-ratory specialist doing his midnight thing in his own backyard pool, immediately sensed Toby's dilemma and sailed in to save him. He vaulted over the fence and jumped in Toby's pool, only to realize that he then had a problem. He, the doctor, only weighed 135 pounds. But he struggled and pushed, finally maneuvering his new neigh-bor to the edge of the pool. However, he couldn't lift Toby out, only his head and shoulders.

The specialist then pro-ceeded to administer artificial respiration to Toby, and with each depression a stream of water gushed from Toby's mouth. This pro-cedure continued for several minutes before the doctor noticed a stranger in cover-alls standing at the corner of Toby's house, munching on an apple and observing.

"You're doin' that all wrong, you know," he re-marked nonchalantly.

"All wrong? What do you mean?" the almost breathless doctor replied. "I'll have you know that I've been engaged in the field of respiratory therapy for 17 years." And, he kept pushing on Toby's back. And the water kept spewing from his mouth.

"Don't care 'bout that," the coverall clad intruder said as he took another bite out of his apple. "I still say you're doin' it all wrong."

"Well, who are you? Are you a doctor?"

"Nope, I'm a plumber, And I can tell you this. If you don't get that fella' all the way out of the water, you're gonna' pump the pool dry!"

◆ ◆ ◆ ◆ ◆

The South Georgia water-melon farmer had tried, in vain, to put a stop to the repeated theft of his watermelons. Almost every night after going to bed the farmer would hear the drone of a truck motor in the vicinity of his watermelon patch, followed by a silence for several minutes. Then, he would hear the truck crank up and drive away. The next morning he would walk to his watermelon patch only to find that several of his prized melons had been stolen.

The farmer put signs on the gate leading to the watermelon patch, "Do Not Enter," "Posted, No Trespassing," "Keep Out," and so on, to no avail. His watermelons continued to be stolen by unknown culprits.

Finally, he came up with what he thought was a foolproof sign that would surely stop the thefts. He made the sign and hung it on the gate late in the afternoon. In bold letters he had printed,

---

"Beware!

One Of The Watermelons

In This Patch Has Been

Poisoned With Cyanide!"

Satisfied that he had solved his watermelon theft problem, he retired early to get a good night's sleep. But about 2 a.m. he was awakened by a familiar sound, the drone of a truck motor coming from the vicinity of his watermelon patch. He listened intently as the sound stopped, but started again in a matter of seconds. He smiled contentedly as he heard that truck drive away, confident that his sign had worked, and said to his wife,

"Well, I fixed them watermelon thieves this time, honey," and immediately went back to sleep.

The next morning he rose bright and early, anxious to get to his watermelon patch. Upon arrival, he observed that his latest sign was still intact, hanging on the gate. But, to his dismay, the wording had been changed to read like this:

> Now Two "Beware!
> ~~One~~ Of The Watermelons
> Have
> In This Patch ~~Has~~ Been
> Poisoned With Cyanide!"

◆ ◆ ◆ ◆ ◆

One fine Carolina evening a Mrs. George Wood, now deceased, called a Dr. Marvin Satterfield, a veterinarian in Edonton, from her home in Chowan County. It was about her mule, Horace. She was upset and said: "Doctor, Horace is sick and I wish you would come out and take a look at him."

The sun was setting, but there was still plenty of daylight to see by. After asking a few questions and hearing the answers, Dr. Satterfield said: "Oh, Fannie Lamb, it's after six o'clock and I'm eating supper. Give him a dose of mineral oil and if he isn't all right in the morning, phone me and I'll come and take a look at your mule."

She wanted to know how to give the mule the mineral oil and the doctor said it should be given through a funnel. Mrs. Wood protested that the mule might bite her and Dr. Satterfield, a bit exasperated, said, "You're a farm woman and you know about these things, Fannie Lamb. Give it to him in the other end."

Fannie Lamb went down to the barn and there stood Horace, moaning and groaning and banging his head. He certainly looked sick. She searched for a funnel but the nearest thing to one she could find was Uncle Bill's fox hunting horn, hanging on the wall of the barn. This was a beautiful gold-plated instrument with silver tassels.

She took the horn and affixed it properly. Horace paid no attention, and she was encouraged. Then she reached up on the shelf where the medicines for the farm animals were kept. Instead of picking up the mineral oil bottle, however, she grabbed a bottle of turpentine and poured a liberal dose of it into the horn.

Horace raised his head with a sudden jerk and stood dead still at attention for maybe three seconds. Then he let out a squeal that could be heard a mile down the road. He reared up on his hind legs, brought his front legs down, knocked out one side of the barn, cleared a six-foot fence and started down the road at a mad gallop. And since Horace was in pain, every few jumps he made, the horn would blow.

Now then, all the hound dogs in the neighborhood knew that when the horn was blowing, it meant Uncle Bill was going fox hunting. So out on the road they went, following close behind Horace the Mule.

People who witnessed that chase said it was an unforgettable sight. First, Horace, running at top speed and the horn in a most unusual position, the mellow notes issuing therefrom, the silver tassels waving, and the dogs running, jumping and barking joyously.

They passed the home of Old Man Harvey Hogan, who was sitting on his front porch. It was said that Mr. Hogan had not drawn a sober breath in fifteen years. He gazed in fascinated amazement at the sight which unfolded itself before his eyes and couldn't believe what he was seeing. Incidentally, Old Man Harvey Hogan is said now to be head man for Alcoholics Anonymous in the Albermarle section of North Carolina.

By this time it was good and dark. Horace and the dogs were coming to the Inland Waterway. The bridge tender heard the horn blowing frantically and figured that a fast boat was approaching. He hurriedly went out and cranked up the bridge. Horace went kerplunk in the water and, unfortunately, drowned. The pack of dogs also went flying into the water, but they all swam out without much difficulty.

What makes the story doubly interesting is that the bridge tender was also sheriff of Chowan County and was running for reelection at the time. But he managed to get only seven votes, and these were all from kinfolks.

Those who took the trouble to analyze the election votes said the people figured that any man who didn't know the difference between a mule with a horn up his caboose and a boat coming down the Inland Waterway wasn't fit to hold any public office in the county.

Once, before the advent of television, there was a lady who lived in a remote area up in the mountains, completely isolated from the world down below. She was born there and had never been off the mountain. She knew nothing about the Bible, so one of her neighbors felt sorry for her and sent a preacher to her home to get her converted.

When the visiting preacher knocked on her door, the mountain lady came out on the porch; and the preacher asked, "Are you a Christian?"

"No, I'm a Republican," she answered.

"Sister, I'm afraid you're in the dark," said the preacher.

"Yes, I guess I am," she agreed. "I think I'll get John to cut another window when he gets back home."

"Does John fear the Lord?"

"I guess he must," she said, "because he took his shotgun with him when he left."

"I mean, does he have salvation?"

"Yes, he does. He has it pretty bad in his right hip," she allowed.

"Sister, would you like to go to heaven?" asked the preacher.

"I don't really know 'bout that," she said. "John and I have been thinking seriously 'bout leaving here and moving to Texas."

"Sister, do you have any idea why I'm up here today?"

"No, I guess I don't."

"Well, I'm up here in these mountains looking for lost sheep," he said.

"Is that so? Well, I saw three late yesterday afternoon and I told John those sheep were lost," she explained. "But I think they belong to ol' man Mitchell who lives over on the next mountain."

"Well, let me ask you this: Are there any Presbyterians up here in these mountains?"

"Shoot yeah! John caught one last week and I can tell you that I had one heck of a time skinnin' it," she said. "Tough as whit leather, too."

Obviously upset at his inability to get his message through to the mountain lady, the preacher came right to the point, and asked, "Sister, don't you know that Jesus died to save sinners?"

"He did?!" she exclaimed. "I'm real sorry. I didn't even know he was sick. If I had known I would have sent him a jar of jelly."

The preacher turned to leave, but made one more attempt to get through to the mountain lady, "Well Sister, I'll see you in the Promised Land."

"You may see John and the kids, but I don't hardly ever

go nowhere myself," she replied.

♦ ♦ ♦ ♦ ♦

Grady Collins insists this one is true. A few years back he was fishing with his good friend G. C. Hawkins. It was on Sunday morning, and when the church bells began ringing, Grady asked G. C., "Don't it make you feel a little guilty to be here fishing when church is fixin' to start, G. C.?"

G. C. was busy with his line and never looked up as he answered. "Nope. Couldn't have gone to church nohow this morning."

"Why not?"

"My wife's sick."

♦ ♦ ♦ ♦ ♦

This fella' was on a camping trip, and had been in the woods for several days. It was cold and rainy so just before dark he built a fire and commenced to cook supper. He put on a can of water to boil for coffee, and a skillet filled with grease and a couple of pounds of bacon.

The fire was goin' good, the water was boilin', and the bacon was fryin'. As the fella' stood warmin' his hands and anticipatin' his supper, he heard a loud noise in the woods. Sounded like a freight train comin' toward him. Well he looked up an' saw the biggest, meanest lookin' bear he'd ever seen chargin' toward him. And on the bear was the biggest, meanest lookin' man he'd ever seen. An' the man was whippin' that bear with a seven-foot rattlesnake.

'Whoa'! he hollered as he and the bear came slidin' up to the campsite.

The man jumped off the bear, bit the head right off that rattlesnake, and threw him in the creek nearby. Then the man reared back and hit that bear right between the eyes with his fist, knocking the bear out cold. Next, he reached down and grabbed the red-hot coffee can and drank every drop of the boilin' coffee, an' threw the can in the creek. He then reached in with his bare hand, grabbed the frying bacon, ate it all, and then drank the grease. He then tossed the skillet in the creek, reached down an' pulled up a handful of poison ivy, and wiped his face.

He then threw cold water in the bear's face to revive him, reached down and grabbed another rattlesnake, climbed up on the bear, and again began whipping the bear with the snake and yellin', 'Yaaahhh! Giddyup, there'!

As the unknown and uninvited visitor roared out of the campsite, he yelled back over his shoulder: 'Thanks a lot, friend! I hate to eat an' run, but I gotta' git goin'! You see, they's a real BAAAAAADD son-of-a-gun chasin' me!"

♦ ♦ ♦ ♦ ♦

Many Yankees don't realize that some counties in the South are "dry." Dry means that you can't buy liquor in the county. Sometimes it means they don't want you even drinking the stuff.

The traveling salesman pulled into a small town in a dry southern county one hot July afternoon and asked the hotel clerk where he might get a drink of whiskey.

"Can't. This here's a dry county. Only whiskey in town is at Doc Lunsford's office. He keeps it for snake bites. Course you can go on down to Doc's office, but it's mighty late in the afternoon," the clerk told him.

"What do you mean?" asked the salesman.

"Well, Doc ain't got but one snake, and by this time of the day he's plumb tuckered out what with all the salesmen we get in this town."

SOME SELECTED SOUTHERN SUPERSTITIONS

I guess most of us are just a tad superstitious, at least to the point where we don't take unnecessary chances. You know, better safe than sorry.

I really don't go along with that seven year's bad luck baloney if you break a mirror, though. Heck, I knew a man in Waycross, Georgia, who broke one and he didn't have seven year's bad luck at all. He was run over by a train and killed the day after he broke it.

Here is a list of southern superstitions I've heard all my life:

• If you sweep dirt out of the house on Friday, the house will burn down.

• Wash your hair in the first rain of May, and it will grow faster.

• Cross your eyes and jump over a ditch at midnight, and your eyes will stay crossed forever.

• Eat blackeyed peas and hog jowl (Hopping John) on New Year's Day, and you'll have good luck all year.

• Step on a crack and break your mother's back.

• See a cardinal, make a wish, and pinch someone to make it come true.

• Make a wish on a redbird before it flies, and your wish will come true.

• Sleep with a mirror under your pillow, and you will see your future husband.

• When a man's second toe is longer than his big toe, he will be henpecked.

• If a bride goes to the altar with some salt in her pocket, she will always be happy.

• Cats playing with their tails means that bad weather isn't far off.

• If the sun sets behind a cloud on Wednesday night, there will be rain before Sunday.

• When the leaves turn

up, it will rain shortly.

• When fish jump above the water, look for rain.

• Run into a cobweb, and you'll get a letter.

• If your palm itches, you are going to get some money.

• If your nose itches, it means you are going to have company.

• Carry in your pocket a button you've found, and it will bring you good luck.

• Walking on the other side of a post from a friend will bring on a quarrel, unless you say "bread and butter."

• Snakes will not come around a place where gourds are growing.

• Killing a ladybug brings much bad luck.

• Weeds won't grow back if cut in March during the dark of the moon.

• It will bring much bad luck if you sleep on new, unwashed sheets.

• To become beautiful, get behind a door and eat a chicken foot.

• If you put the hand of a sleeping person in water, he will name his sweetheart and answer any question you ask him.

• You'll get a headache if you put your left shoe on before your right.

• A woman who drops her apron will lose a friend.

• If your left foot itches, you will walk where you're not welcome.

• Look under a bed, and you'll never marry.

• It's bad luck to lean a broom against a bed.

• When it rains on June 2, there will be no blackberries.

• If someone sweeps under your feet, you'll never marry.

• If your initials spell a word, you'll become rich.

• When hornet's nests are low, it will be a cold winter; when they're high, winter will be mild.

• If your shoestring becomes untied, someone is talking about you.

• Shaking hands over a fence is unlucky.

• Pull three hairs from your dog's tail and put them under the doorsteps, and your dog will not stray from home.

• You'll have to take each stitch out with your nose if you sew on Sunday.

• If it rains and the sun shines at the same time, it means that the devil is beating his wife with a dishpan.

• Those who have teeth growing wide apart will be travelers.

• When you see a flash of lightning, count as fast as

you can until it thunders. The number you get is how many miles away the lightning has struck.

• Dream about milk, and there will be an increase in your family. Dream about broken eggs, and your troubles are past.

• Sweeping after dark will bring sorrow to your heart.

• Forget to wash a skillet, and you can expect a guest for the next meal.

• It's good luck for a butterfly to light on your shoulder.

• Plant cotton among your cucumbers, and insects will not attack your cucumbers.

• If two people bump heads when they're bending over, they'll sleep together that night.

• If you swim in the ocean on January 1, you won't be sick all year.

• Bake rough cornbread and your husband's face will be rough.

• When your tooth falls out, don't stick your tongue in the hole or the new one will turn to gold.

• When you drop a comb, turn the teeth down or stomp on it and make a wish.

• A wish made in a bed that's never been slept in will come true.

• The first thunder of spring wakes up the snakes and tells you winter is gone.

• If your skirt turns up, you'll catch a sweetheart.

• You can be sure of rough weather if the grape or pecan crop is heavy.

• If you can see the sunshine through a man's ears, he's a rascal and can't be trusted.

• To test a girl's disposition, stretch a piece of her hair. If it curls up, she's high-tempered; and the tighter the curl, the worse her temper is.

• If you pass between two women while walking, you'll have bad luck. Pass between two men, and you'll have good luck.

• Whistle in bed, and you'll cry before the next night.

• A whistling woman, or a hen that crows, has her way wherever she goes.

• Get your hair cut in March, and you'll lose a horse.

• Always step into a court room on your right foot when you have business there.

• A woman with short fingers makes a good manager.

• If you sneeze before breakfast, you'll see your sweetheart before Saturday night.

- It causes bad luck if you take an old broom into a new house.
- It's bad luck to take up ashes from the fireplace during the Christmas season.
- Cut your fingernails before breakfast on Monday morning, and you'll get a present before the week is over.
- If a fly flies around your face continually, a stranger hopes to meet you.
- An owl's hoot around midnight is a sign that somebody in the family will have an accident. To stop the accident from happening, turn an old shoe upside down.
- It's bad luck to climb over anybody in bed.

◆ ◆ ◆ ◆ ◆

And remember this: In the South, it is perfectly permissible to utter any untruth your little heart desires, just as long as you have your fingers crossed.

NAMES ARE THE NAME OF THE GAME

Names are in bountiful supply in Dixie; they must be because a large portion of the redneck population sport two in addition to the last name, especially the girls.

Here are 40 of the most popular girls' names in the South:

1. Martha Ann
2. Robbie Nell
3. Brenda Sue
4. Allie Mae
5. Bobbie Jean
6. Margaret Ann
7. Johnnie Faye
8. Betty Ann
9. Donna Rae
10: Kitty Marie
11. Ellie Mae
12. Sarah Ann
13. Wanda Kay
14. Mary Nell
15. Sally Ann
16. Effie Mae
17. Lisa Ann
18. Mary Jane
19. Elizabeth Ann
20. Ida Jane
21. Peggy Sue
22. Betty Rose
23. Mary Frances
24. Dixie Faye
25. Barbara Ann
26. Bonnie Sue
27. Jo Ann
28. Bessie Mae
29. Connie Faye
30. Norma Jean
31. Mary Lou
32. Betty June
33. Bertie Faye
34. Nellie Rose
35. Emmy Lou
36. Martha Sue
37. Betty Jo
38. Mary Ida
39. Lisa Marie
40. Patricia Ann

The boys, too, sport double names way down south. Here are some of the more common ones, along with some initials that are so popular:

1. Bobby Jack		21. C. L. (Barfield)
2. Joe Frank		22. C. D. (Etheridge)
3. Johnny Mack		23. M. L. (Reid)
4. Billy Bob		24. J. D. (Brown)
5. Jimmy Lee		25. W. L. (Wilkes)
6. Charley Joe		26. M. C. (Darsey)
7. Robert Earl		27. J. B. (Allen)
8. Bobby Joe		28. C. W. (Anderson)
9. Freddie Lee		29. O. K. (Tanner)
10. Benny Earl		30. K. L. (Yates)
11. John Robert		31. C. R. (Roberts)
12. Jim Tom		32. J. R. (Ewing)
13. Tommy Lee		33. J. J. (Walker)
14. Grady Jack		34. D. L. (Causey)
15. Billy Gene		35. T. Z. (Lanier)
16. Bobby Ray		36. T. L. (Tuten)
17. Willie Jack		37. J. B. (Burch)
18. Tony Jack		38. J. T. (Trapnell)
19. Bobby Frank		39. U. S. (Jones)
20. Henry Lee		40. O. B. (Johnson)

Of course, there is a strain of rednecks known neither by first names or initials, but by nickname. They wouldn't answer to anything else. The more recognizable ones are:

1. Bubba	7. Bully
2. Buster	8. Bear
3. Hoss	9. Booger
4. Slick	10. Hawkeye
5. Buddy	11. Dude
6. Snake	12. Bulldog

SECTION FIVE

MUSIC AND ENTERTAINMENT

SYMPHONY OF THE SOUTHLAND

A fella' can do two things with country music. He can listen to it, or he can dance to it. I well remember the first time I danced to it. The year was 1941.

Being the son of a preacher and raised in the shadow of the steeple, I never really had the chance to learn much about dancing as a youngster, but I did try. Peer pressure, you know.

I went to my first dance in Luvale, a small community located half way between Lumpkin and Columbus. The girl whose mama owned the only juke in town invited me.

I was fuzzy-faced and fourteen. I shaved three times before the dance that Saturday night, using my daddy's razor, and looked more like a butchered hog than a dashing troubador bent on tripping the light fantastic. And you can accentuate the word *tripping*.

In preparation for my debut, I practiced all Saturday afternoon in front of the bathroom mirror, using a plunger for a partner. And I might add that the plunger was built better than most of the girls at the dance. Well, it really wasn't a dance. They didn't have dances in Luvale. It was a "daintz," and there's a definite difference, Delsey.

The music, always country, was provided by a juke box in the corner next to the drink box that featured such classics of the early 40s as "Down Yonder," "Walking the Floor Over You," "Have You Ever Been Lonely," "Soldier's Last Letter," "By The Light of the Silvery Moon," and "Wreck on the Highway."

In 1941 the songs went for a nickel each, six for a quarter. But the juke box had a sensitive spot that one of the boys knew about where if you tapped it just right the songs would keep coming.

I rode to the dance with my best friend, Dan Ford. He was a good dancer, but the girl he took to the dance moved around the floor like a petrified pine. Dan kept bribing me with R. C. Colas to dance with her so he could trip around the corn-meal-covered floor with Marie Parks, the Ginger Rogers of Luvale. Man, that girl could flat dance!

I gave Dan's date Kate a nickname that night that stuck with her right on through high school: "Plunger." And the last I heard of her she was operating a bulldozer in the Columbus area.

"Goose" Geeslin was at the dance, too. "Goose" was only slightly smaller than a water tank, and tough. They didn't nobody at Stewart County High School mess with "Goose," who had light red hair and an over-abundance of freckles all over. He weighed in at around 210, all muscle. No doubt about it, "Goose" Geeslin would cut you.

For most of the night "Goose" sat by the drink box and watched. He watched Marie Parks. She didn't take a dance step all night long

that he didn't see. When she sat down, he zeroed in on her. "Goose" was sweet on Marie in his own way.

On into the night the juke was playing a soft, sweet tune, "By the Light of the Silvery Moon," and "Goose" was staring holes through Marie.

"Why don't you ask her to dance, Goose?" I asked him.

"Uh-uh. Can't do that," he said.

"Why not?"

"Jus' can't, tha's all," he growled.

"Aw, go on an' ask her," I prodded.

"Nope. Can't do that for two reasons," he allowed. "If I ask her to daintz an' she says 'yes" I'll be in a mess, an' if she says 'no' I'll be in a mess."

"Why? What do you mean?"

"Well, it's like this," he said. "If she says 'yes,' I can't daintz; An' if she says 'no,' I'll more'n likely knock hell out of her!"

Going to my first dance at the ripe old age of fourteen was one thing, but going to a country music concert in 1984 at the ripe old age of 56 was another. I thoroughly enjoyed it, but what I saw that day was an eye-opener. The performing group was

Alabama, the best in the business. Come with me, if you will, to the concert that was staged in the Macon Coliseum.

Is there life after *Alabama*? The devoted fans of the musical group, "Entertainers of the Year" in 1982 and 1983 by vote of the Country Music Association, aren't real sure. They think that when you die you go to Fort Payne, Alabama, home turf of the colorful and talented youngsters.

The drive to Macon was very pleasant, until I approached the Coliseum entrance. The line of cars resembled an automotive assembly plant. I by-passed the parking lot and managed to find a parking place somewhere in the vicinity of Atlanta, 89 miles away.

After a nice, but long, hike I entered the Coliseum and located my seat. A great seat. Nothing but the best. It was in the last row (row 50), about two steps removed from a concessions stand and behind a post. I could hear *Alabama*, but I couldn't see them. Of course, the people up near Atlanta where my car was parked could probably hear them, too. And I'm sure they had better seats.

With a 45-minute wait until the show was scheduled to start, I enjoyed watching the crowd file in. It consisted of long ones, short ones, skinny ones, fat ones, pretty ones, ugly ones, young ones, old ones—with one thing in common. They loved *Alabama*. And I saw more blue jeans than Levi Strauss, Gloria Vanderbilt, Calvin Klein, Lee, Chic, and Mr. Wrangler ever dreamed of. Tight? Friends and neighbors, most of the female jeans were Vidalia onion skin tight. One girl, about nineteen, was sporting a pair so tight that her appendectomy scar was plainly visible. If they had busted we'd have all been killed!

If there has ever been 10,000 country music lovers gathered together under one roof and ready to party, it was the Sunday afternoon throng in Macon Coliseum. You could feel it as the 3:00 P.M. starting time approached.

About 2:47 P.M. the hand-clapping began. This was followed by foot-stomping at 2:55. Then, the announcement came: "The start of the show has been changed to 3:15 to allow those trying to park additional time to get inside," the public address man said.

"Why the heck didn't they park up near Atlanta and walk, like I did?" I asked of no one in particular. And no one in particular answered. They were too busy clapping their hands and stomping their feet.

Shortly after 3:00 P.M., a young couple wearing blue jeans arrived and took their seats in front of me on row 49. The male was holding what appeared to be about a three-month old baby boy, dressed out in a miniature *Alabama* T-shirt.

Once seated, the female reached into one of those carry-all bags, pulled out a baby bottle, and handed it to her husband, who was holding the baby. The little fan knew exactly what to do with it, and in a few minutes it was empty.

Of course, Daddy knew what to do. He placed the child's head on his shoulder and patted his back gently, then firmer. Baby came through with flying colors.

"Buuuuuuuurrrrppp!"

Did I say the crowd was in a party mood? You better believe it, because when the baby boy burped three couples seated in the immediate vicinity got up and danced.

It was a dadgummed good concert. That *Alabama* can flat get it on.

Saturday nights are usually reserved for dining and dancing, but not always. There are households in Dixie where country music reigns supreme on Saturday nights with the radio tuned to WSM in Nashville, Tennessee, the Grand Ole Opry station. Turning the dial to 650-AM is automatic. Yep, Saturday nights are syrup and biscuits and country ham and red-eye gravy and grits and Grand Ole Opry nights.

The folks in Dixie grew up and swore by the likes of Red Foley, Cowboy Copas, Carl Smith, Webb Pierce, Roy Acuff, Hank Snow, Ernest Tubb, Rod Brasfield, "The Duke of Paducah," Minnie Pearl, "Little Jimmy" Dickens, Hank Williams, Eddy Arnold, Chet Atkins, "Stringbean," Homer and Jethro, The Carter Family, Johnny Cash, Patsy Cline, Tom T. Hall, Lester Flatt, The Jordanaires, Bill Monroe and The Bluegrass Boys, Uncle Dave Macon, Kitty Wells, The Bailes Brothers, Lonzo and Oscar and a host of others.

Hell, they were family! Country music sends out a message. The performers sing words, not lyrics. They sing words that mean something and echo a message a fella' can understand and relate to. They'll make you cry, and laugh; remember and forget; cuss and pray.

My good friend Lewis Grizzard, premier columnist for the *Atlanta Constitution,* is a good ol' boy from Moreland, Georgia. He's a dyed-in-the-wool country music fan and will bring tears to your eyes when he relates how country music saved his life in the desolate, cold and unfriendly atmosphere of Chicago.

"I was homesick and lonely. My wife had backed a truck up to the apartment and cleaned me out. She took everything but the blame, including my dog. An' I'll tell you this, any woman who'll take y'r dog'll cutcha'. I realized that the only person who loved me was my mama, an' she was 800 miles away in Georgia. So I reached for the only thing I had left, my country music albums. I selected one at random, without looking at the title, and dropped it on the turntable of my stereo. The reassuring words rendered forth as I gazed out my window at a cold, snowy day in Chicago, 'You tore my heart out an' stomped that sucker flat'."

Two other Grizzard favorites are, "Don't Give Me No Plastic Saddle, Baby . . . I Want To Feel That Leather When I Ride," and "Mama's Cookin', Daddy's Jukin' . . . An' The Baby's Eatin' The Fly Swatter Again."

Still another lifelong lover of country music is Ludlow Porch from Snellville, Georgia. Ludlow is known and loved by all as "Mr. Radio" in Atlanta where he holds forth daily doing a five-hour talk show on WSB-AM.

"Shoot, I was a country music fan long before it was fashionable," Porch allows. "Heck, I was listenin' to country music when Dolly Parton was still wearin' a trainin' bra; when Porter Waggoner could only afford one sequin; when Merle Haggard was a trusty. What I'm sayin' is, I was a country music fan when Donnie and Marie wore braces on their teeth, an' when Oral Roberts was goin' to a chiropractor. I love country music because country music singers sing words that tug at your heartstrings; words that make you want to cry; words that make you want to go right out an' beat up a Commie. I'm talkin' 'bout beautiful, meaningful words like, 'Our Marriage Was A Failure, But Our Divorce Ain't Workin' Out Either', 'Hold My Beer, Leon, While I Knee Jane Fonda', and 'Bobby Joe, Yore Wife Is Cheatin' On Us Again'."

'Nother thing, down here in Dixie we have country music rednecks, male and female, who tithe with regularity. Ten percent of everything they make goes in the jukebox. Their theory is that "if Willie Nelson says it, it's true."

What, really, is country music? Just this:

Country music is more than entertainment, more than pickin' and grinnin', more than two-for-a-quarter selections on a juke box in some remote honky-tonk or truck stop. It is more than a concert in the local high school auditorium, more than Willie Nelson going one-on-one on the radio with an over-the-road trucker at midnight bound from Atlanta to Houston. It is more than a Saturday night dance at the VFW, more than music to work and play by.

In Dixie, country music is a way of life, and to some almost a religion. It is just as southern as grits, hot biscuits, and redeye gravy. It bares the facts of life, the good and bad. It is music that the common everyday working man can relate to. Many country songs are confessions; others are mere revelations.

If country music is a way of life for many in the south, it is also a journey. I know. It is a good and reliable companion that has traveled with me for more than 50 years.

SUCCESS IN MUSIC CITY, U.S.A.

My friend Robbie Nell Bell recently quit her waitress job at Mel's Juke, had the water pump fixed on her '73 Ford, and moved to Nashville. She's taken up writin' country songs full-time.

She called (collect) from Nashville one Saturday night after the Grand Ole Opry from a Nashville spot called the Ace of Spades.

"How in the world are you, Robbie Nail?" I asked.

"Fine, Chief, jus' fine," she said. "Writin' country songs an' makin' money faster'n a bootlegger. Even think' 'bout gittin' married agin soon's my boyfriend, Roy, gits his d'vorce from that ol' Margie."

"Well, congratulations. What took you to Nashville?" I asked.

"Y'member that song I wrote that Bobby an' th' Rattlesnakes recorded in Waycross 'bout two years

ago, "Papa Died and Mama Cried, 'Cause the Insurance Had Done Lapsed'?"

"Right, I remember, A real tear-jerker," I said.

"Wail, that's whut started th' whole thaing," she said. "Roy, tha's my boyfriend, heard it an' his band, Roy's Ramblers, recorded it. Roy done th' saingin', naturally, an' it became a big hit. So now, I write 'em an' Roy saings 'em. He gives me seven dollars f'r ever one I write."

"I'm proud of you. Have you written very many?" I asked.

"Shoot I reckon! A whole 'baccer sheet full," she bellowed, "I had a real big 'un right after Thanksgiving las' year when my brother's wife run off with th' Roto-Rooter man."

"What was the name of it?"

"You mean you ain't heard it? It's called, 'I Stuffed Her

Turkey and She Cooked My Goose,'" she said. "I tell you what, I'll jus' send all of 'em down to you an' you can be my Georgia agent. How 'bout that?" she giggled.

"Great! Send 'em on down. you have lots of fans in this area," I told her.

I'm not sure you're ready for this, but here is the list of songs written by Robbie Nail Bail, fum Almer, that arrived in the morning mail:

• "When I'm Alone I'm in Bad Company"
• "A Sad Song Don't Care Whose Heart It Breaks"
• "I Wouldn't Take Her to a Dogfight, but I Know She'd Win if I Did"
• "I May Fall Again, but I'll Never Get Up This Slow"
• "You're the Busiest Memory in Town"
• "Your Face Is Familiar, but I Forget the Name"
• "You Don't Have to Go Home, Baby, but You Can't Stay Here"
• "It's Easy to Find an Unhappy Woman Till I Start Looking for Mine"
• "The More I Think of You, the Less I Think of Me"
• "Don't Cry Down My Back, Baby, You Might Rust My Spurs"
• "I Can't Afford to Half My Half Again"
• "The Bridge Washed Out, I Can't Swim, and My Baby's on the Other Side of the River"
• "Forever, for Us, Wasn't Nearly as Long as We Planned On"
• "I Got to Her House Just in Time to be Late"
• "I'm Afraid to Come Home Early Without Warning Her First"
• "My Wife Ran Off with My Best Friend—And I Sure Do Miss Him"
• "Send Her a Dozen Roses, and Pour Four for Me"
• "He's Walking in My Tracks, but He Can't Fill My Shoes"
• "She's Gone, and She Took Everything but the Blame"
• "I Can't Believe I Gave Up 'Good Mornin' Darling' and 'We Love You Daddy,' for This"
• "I'd Rather Be Picked Up Here Than to Be Put Down at Home"
• "When the Phone Don't Ring, You'll Know It's Me That Ain't Calling"
• "If You Want to Keep the Beer Real Cold, Put It Next to My Ex-Wife's Heart"
• "I Need Somebody Bad Tonight 'Cause I Just Lost Somebody Good Today"
• "The Score Is: Liars

One—Believers Zero"

- "I'm Ashamed to Be Here, but Not Ashamed Enough to Leave"
- "How Can Six-year-old Whiskey Beat a Thirty-two-year-old Man?"
- "She's Waiting on Tables While Waiting for the Tables to Turn"
- "Now That She's Got Me Where She Wants Me, She Don't Want Me"
- "I Can't Even Do Wrong Right No More"
- "The Devil Is a Woman in a Short Red Dress"

- "She Ain't Much to See, but She Looks Good Through the Bottom of a Glass"
- "I Done 'Bout Lived Myself to Death"
- "It's Bad When You Get Caught with the Goods"
- "Remember to Remind Me I'm Leaving"
- "It Took a Hell of a Man to Take My Ann, but it Sure Didn't Take Him Long to Do It"
- "Them What Ain't Got Can't Lose"
- "I'm Sick and Tired of Waking Up Sick and Tired"

DEER HUNTING

Hunting is one of a redneck's favorite activities. But, as with all things, there's a right way to do it.

◆　◆　◆　◆　◆

Two New Jersey Americans went deer hunting for the first time near Willacoochee. One killed a big buck just after daylight and they began dragging it by the tail to the pickup truck more than a mile away.

A Willacoochee native saw them as they struggled past his stand, almost out of breath. They were within sight of the pickup, about 300 yards away.

"I b'leeve you boys'd have a easier time of it draggin' that buck by the horns," he told them.

They heeded his suggestion, walked to the deer's head, took a firm grip on his 12-point rack and began dragging. After thirty minutes they stopped to catch their breath.

"That fellow was right," one said. "Sure is a heck of a lot easier to pull this deer by the horns than by the tail, ain't it?"

"Yeah," said the other, "but have you noticed how far away from the truck we're getting?"

◆　◆　◆　◆　◆

Now I'm not saying that the following is the right way to do it, but show me a hunter who won't admit to having at least one deer huntin' experience like it, and I'll show you one who makes me leery of his honesty.

"DIARY OF A DEER HUNTER"

- 1:00 A.M.:　SATURDAY. Alarm clock rings.
- 2:00 A.M.:　Hunting partners arrive and drag you out of bed.
- 2:30 A.M.:　Throw everything in pickup except kitchen sink.
- 3:00 A.M.:　Leave for the deep woods.
- 3:15 A.M.:　Drive back home to pick up gun.
- 3:30 A.M.:　Drive like crazy to get to woods before daylight.
- 4:00 A.M.:　Set up camp . . . forgot stupid tent.
- 4:30 A.M.:　Head into woods, climb tree, get in stand.
- 5:15 A.M.:　Take first shot of antifreeze.
- 5:20 A.M.:　Attempt to light cigarette with wet match.
- 5:31 A.M.:　Walk back to pickup to use cigarette lighter.
- 6:00 A.M.:　Back in tree—second shot of antifreeze.
- 6:05 A.M.:　Spot eight deer while lighting second cigarette from butt of first cigarette.
- 6:06 A.M.:　Drop cigarette, take aim through scope and squeeze trigger.
- 6:06-08:　"CLICK"
- 6:07 A.M.:　Load gun while watching eight deer disappear over hill.
- 8:00 A.M.:　Head back to camp for breakfast.
- 9:00 A.M.:　Still looking for camp. Recognize tree you climbed out of an hour earlier.
- 9:12 A.M.:　Try again to light cigarette with wet match.
- 9:14 A.M.:　Rub two sticks together in vain attempt to start fire. Realize why you never advanced beyond rank of Tenderfoot in Boy Scouts.
- 10:00 A.M.:　Face the fact that you don't know where you are.
- NOON:　FIRE GUN REPEATEDLY FOR HELP. EAT WILD BERRIES FOR LUNCH.
- 12:15 P.M.:　The eight deer come back . . . CLICK . . . All out of bullets.
- 12:20 P.M.:　Strange feeling in stomach.
- 12:30 P.M.:　Realize you ate poison berries for lunch.
- 12:45 P.M.:　RESCUED.

- **12:55 P.M.:** Rushed to hospital to have stomach pumped out.
- **3:00 P.M.:** Arrive back in camp.
- **3:30 P.M.:** Leave camp and walk back to deer stand.
- **4:00 P.M.:** Walk back to camp for bullets.
- **4:01 P.M.:** Load gun and leave camp again.
- **5:00 P.M.:** Empty gun on squirrel that's been bugging you.
- **6:00 P.M.:** Arrive back at camp . . . see deer grazing in camp.
- **6:01 P.M.:** Load gun.
- **6:01:13:** FIRE GUN.
- **6:02 P.M.:** ONE DEAD PICKUP TRUCK.
- **6:05 P.M.:** Hunting partner returns to camp dragging deer with 13-point rack you missed at 6:02 P.M.
- **6:06 P.M.:** Suppress strong desire to shoot hunting partner.
- **6:07 P.M.:** Stumble over hunting partner's deer and fall into campfire.

- 6:15 P.M.: Take pickup—leave hunting partner and his deer in woods.
- 6:25 P.M.: Radiator boils over due to hole shot in motor block.
- 6:26 P.M.: Start walking.
- 6:30 P.M.: Trip over stump, stumble and fall. Drop gun in mud. Retrieve it and keep walking.
- 6:35 P.M.: Meet bear head-on.
- 6:35:01: Aim and fire at bear. Blow up gun barrel that's plugged with mud.
- 6:35:04: MESSED UP PANTS.
- 6:35:08: Cast gun down and climb up nearby tree.
- 9:05 P.M.: Bear departs. Climb down out of tree. Retrieve gun and wrap around tree. Start walking.
- MIDNIGHT: Home at last. Light cigarette with dry match and pour third shot (double) of antifreeze.
- 1:00 P.M.: SUNDAY. Watch football on TV while slowly tearing hunting license in little pieces.

CHECKERS

Last Saturday I straddled my motorcycle and headed south. Nowhere in particular, just south. Actually, what I had in mind was a country store, Vienna sausage, saltines and a Coke (in a bottle, please); maybe a cinnamon roll.

While I didn't know where I was going, I knew I had two days to get there and back. I watched city limit signs click off as I rolled down 341. McRae, Scotland, Towns, Lumber City, (Coffee in Lumber City). Hazlehurst, Baxley, Surrency, Jesup.

In Jesup I studied the road signs while waiting for a traffic light to change. One caught my eye: "Ludowici. 14 miles." Why not? Hadn't been to Ludowici in ten years. (A little advice right here: When you pass Ludowici, pass Ludowici.)

I turned around in front of the Long County Courthouse and rode back ten miles to the Altamaha River and a country store near Doctortown. It had a gas pump. Time for a pit stop.

THE BIG GAME IN DOCTORTOWN

The sign said, "Doc's Place." Made sense to me so I pulled in, parked and dismounted. A dog, blocking the doorway, could have cared less had I arrived on a battleship. I stepped over him and went inside.

Four men were watching two more play checkers. Sugar Bowl? Forget it. Checkers is the big game in Doctortown, every day. They turned in unison, looked, and turned back to the checkerboard.

Memories flashed fast and furious, to my grandpa's country store in Hancock

County back in the 30s. Checkers was the big game there, too. Sugar Bowl? Between the gravy and mashed potatoes on Grandma's table.

There's just something about country stores and checkers. Grandpa would always spit tobacco juice, Brown's Mule tobacco juice, right before making a big jump. Stand to his right and you jumped, too. Grandpa always spit to the right. Even his brown bulldog, Scrappy, knew that. Scrappy was a white bulldog when Grandpa got him.

Regulars at Grandpa's were Lunce Brake, George Rocker and Sam Barksdale. They played with Nehi caps on a homemade board. Claude Hill, the rural mail carrier from Sparta, played if he was ahead of schedule. Sometimes, even if he wasn't, he'd stop and watch for a spell, always standing to Grandpa's left. Claude Hill had a good memory; better than Scrappy.

WIPED OUT BY ROSCOE

I watched the game for a few minutes, standing to the rear just to be on the safe side. Nobody spoke to me until the game was over. Doc won.

"Howdy. You play checkers?" Doc asked.

"Used to, a long time ago," I replied.

"C'mon, set y'sef down here an' play ol' Roscoe. Y'can beat 'im with your eyes closed," Doc assured me.

Roscoe said nothing, just nodded in the direction of the chair, I obliged, sat down, and it took ol' Roscoe

less than two minutes to wipe me out. I never got a king. I couldn't have beaten him if his eyes were closed.

I guess there's an opportunist in every crowd and Doctortown is no exception. He was perched on a bag of chicken feed.

"Play ya' for a dollar," he offered.

"Lay off, Shorty! Ya' wanna' play? I'll play ya' and betcha' ten to one," Doc said.

"Shoot! I ain't no fool," Shorty replied.

Nobody called his bet, thereby verifying the sanity of the other four.

THIS WOULD BE A DREAM MATCH

I thanked Doc and his checker-playing pals for their hospitality, bought two dollars worth of gas, Vienna sausage, saltines and a Coke (in a bottle) and hit the road. He was out of cinnamon rolls.

The dog was as enthusiastic about my departure as he was my arrival. I think I could have beaten him, with his eyes open. (In fact, I'd bet twenty to one on it, Shorty.)

I rode to Surrency before pulling off under a tree to eat and listen to the news. I flipped on the radio and sprawled out under the tree. And I thought about Grandpa. . . .

What I wouldn't give to stand to one side, the left side, and watch Grandpa, Doc, Roscoe, Shorty, Lunce Brake, George Rocker and Sam Barksdale square off on the checkerboard. Claude Hill? His substitute would be carrying the mail that day. I'd bet twenty to one on it.

THE RATTLESNAKE ROUNDUP

Legend has it that St. Patrick, the fifth century Christian missionary, drove all the snakes from Ireland. If the legend is true, and St. Patrick did indeed drive all the snakes from Ireland, I have news. After 1,500 years I've found 'em. At least I found 346 of 'em recently. They were in Claxton, Georgia, at the Fourteenth Annual Evans County Rattlesnake Roundup, along with 15,000 snake enthusiasts.

Now I've known for a long time that rednecks often have a fascination with rattlesnakes. But 15,000 of 'em? Shoot! I don't know which was the most dangerous, the people or the snakes.

Here I am on the shady side of 50 and thought I had seen about all there was to see in the way of spectaculars. I mean, what else could an old country boy hope for? I'd seen a soap box derby, a cock fight in the Philippine Islands, the World Skeet Shooting Championships in Pontiac, Michigan, the Olympic ski jump trials in Ishpeming, Michigan, the Indianapolis 500, the Super Bowl, Mardi Gras, two World Series, the Kentucky Derby and the Masters Water Ski Championships at Callaway Gardens. What's left?

A Rattlesnake Roundup? I've spent all my life running from 'em, but I went to find them in Claxton anyway. I wasn't exactly overjoyed at the signs I saw once I hit the city limits. First one said "Hospital," with an arrow pointing straight ahead. The next one was on the lawn of the First United Methodist Church, "Welcome to Rattlesnake Country."

Ever heard of such a thing? A church advertising snakes? My book tells me that man's troubles all started in the first place because of a snake in the Garden of Eden. While my book doesn't say the serpent was a rattlesnake, it doesn't say it wasn't, either.

I drove on to Rattlesnake Roundup headquarters at the Claxton Tobacco Warehouse and entered. That was my first mistake. Within minutes I was ushered through the assembled thousands to the center ring known as the snake pit. Before I knew it, I was inside the snake pit with my trusty camera.

I looked around at the more than 300 rattlesnakes. I watched them coil and listened to them hiss and rattle. I watched grown men reach down and pick up rattlesnakes nearly six feet long and milk venom from their mouths. I was on my knees less than 12 inches away snapping pictures of the pit vipers.

I WON TWO TROPHIES IN ABSENTIA

I wasn't even entered in the roundup competition but won two trophies. I presume they'll be mailed to me because I wasn't around when the awards were presented. It happened this way:

I was crouched next to a flimsy pen holding about 100 rattlesnakes trying to take a picture of one with his head up about ten inches and flipping his (or her) forked tongue out. A guy was simultaneously taking snakes from a nearby flimsy pen and milking them. Well, sir, he dropped one and it fell on the concrete floor not

more than three feet from yours truly. Right then is when I won my first trophy for "Jumping the Highest When a Rattlesnake is Dropped Nearby."

My second first-place trophy, which I hope will arrive in this week's mail, was for "Running Fastest While Wearing Wet Pants With a Nikkormat Camera Strapped Around Your Neck." (I darn near ran over a fella in a wheelchair. Would have, too, if I could have caught up with him.)

Which reminds me of the story of the rural youngster who was sent to the spring by his mother to fetch a pail of water. He returned shortly, as white as the proverbial sheet, holding an empty bucket.

"Where's the water, boy?" his mother questioned.

"Didn't git no water," he puffed.

"Why not?"

"Because there's a big ol' snake in that spring," he said.

"Aw, come on now. You just remember this. That snake is just as scared of you as you are of him," his mother assured him.

"Are you sure about that?" asked the boy.

"Positive," she said.

"Then there ain't no use to go git no water out of that spring."

"Why not?"

"Because it ain't fit to drink!"

SECTION SIX

FEMALE REDNECKS

A LOOK AT THE FEMALE OF THE SPECIES

Sadly, when we make reference to rednecks, most of us think of males. Friend, there are many dyed-in-the-wool, pedigreed and card-carrying female rednecks scattered around. They cover Dixie like kudzu.

The female of the species is a fun-lovin' ol' gal who only wants to know the answer to one question, "Where we partyin' at t'night, Bubba?"

There are three things that a female redneck just flat don't want nobody to mess with: her pool stick, her young'uns an' her man. She'll cutcha' without hesitation if you do.

Her wardrobe will usually consist of jeans, sneakers and boots, a few shirts of varying descriptions and some sort of sweater or jacket. And the jeans must fit skin tight. That's a must.

She smokes Salem Light 100s or Vantage, drinks Coors Light and eats wherever she happens to be at the time. Coffee is a no-no, but she's big on Pepsi, even for breakfast.

She's on a first name basis with all the bartenders and coffee shop short-order cooks and waitresses. She knows the menu by heart and can rattle off the name of every song on the juke box by heart.

She drives about a 1972 Plymouth, with the water pump busted. And it needs tires. Her child support is always three or four months overdue and the rent and light bill needs paying. But there's beer in th' 'frigerator.

She's loyal to her young'uns an' stands by her ol' man in thick an' thin. She goes to see her mama every day.

I think the loyalty of a redneck wife is best illustrated in the classic story of this one, and her redneck hus-

band, who lived way down in South Georgia:

Late one cold afternoon in February, a school bus pulled up in front of their house and tooted the horn. The husband, Buster, reached for his hat and coat and walked out of the house toward the bus. His wife and four children, ages eight months, two, three-and-a-half and five stood in the doorway and watched. Finally, she spoke.

"Buster, you ain't a' goin' to that basketball game down to th' high school, are ya'?"

"Yeah, baby, tha's where I'm headin'," he turned and answered. "Why?"

"But it's cold an' we ain't got no stovewood in th' house, Buster, not a single stick," she pleaded.

Buster pondered her words for a second, then said to her as he stepped into the bus, "But Sugah, I ain't takin' th' axe."

SALLY'S GONNA PARTY ALL NIGHT LONG

It isn't just the guys who stay on the go, though. I know some women who wouldn't stay home Friday and Saturday nights if you chained them to the refrigerator. They'd drag that frost-free sucker right on down to their favorite night spot and "get it on," with the box dragging behind.

Take Sally, for instance. She's a flat (well, not really) goin' out gal.

As the office clock approaches 5:00 P.M. any Friday, Sally starts boogying in her desk chair while finger-tapping on her desk top. And when the big hand reaches twelve and the little hand is on five, watch out! She exits the office like a speed skater, does the Michael Jackson moon walk through the parking lot, and slides under the steering wheel of her little compact gas saver.

Does Sally start the engine, back out, and dig off right away? Hardly. First things first. She turns the radio on, predialed to her favorite station, lights up a Salem Light 100 and then backs out and boogies all the way home, the steering wheel replacing her desk top.

From 5:13 P.M. until 7:00 P.M., Sally takes care of her young'un, whips up a little supper, bathes, slips (Oops! Excuse me, tugs and struggles) into clean jeans, and drops the dirty dishes in the sink, all done while she guzzles a beer and listens to the pregame warm-up that blasts from her AM-FM radio stereo cassette tape player, the only household item, other than the young'un, that she insisted on keeping when her lawyer drew up the divorce agreement after she and Paul split.

About 7:30 P.M., Sally's baby sitter shows up and it's

Friday night game time.

Actually, Sally's Friday night out really begins the moment she steps out of her front door and trips the light fantastic en route to her car, shouting "Yaaaahhhoooo! Gonna' party ALL night long! Le's git it on, baby!"

If, by chance, you've never seen the jeans-clad Sallys of this world in action on the "daintz" floor Friday and Saturday nights, you really ain't lived a full life. And believe me, it's a crying shame what the Sallys put those little pieces of denim through with all their twistin' an' shakin'.

Like my good friend Buttercup Hill, from Route 3, Baxley, says: "If Sally don't start a fire in your basement, your wood's wet."

Then, there's ol' Claude. He hits the goin' out trail on Friday and Saturday nights, too, lookin' for the Sallys of the night beat. And Claude's a loner.

"Shoot! I ain't takin' no girl to no dance. I sorta' like to m'neuver 'round, m'sef," he allows.

You can spot Claude in a flash. He just sorta' rolls inside the place, swaying from side to side, and has more chains hanging around his neck than Houdini. And his shirt is open to his belly-button so they can be seen. He strolls straight to the bar, leans on it, lights a Winston, and commences to survey the pickin's. He's lookin' for Sally.

Once he spots her, does he approach Sally and say, "Pardon me, would you like to dance?"

Negatory. Ol' Claude's smooth-as-black-velvet-approach runs something like, "Gitcha' tail up, gal, an' le's git it on 'fore I change my mind."

Although Claude may look like Buddy Hackett, smell like the Goat Man, and dance like Dr. Frankenstein's monster, in his mind he looks like Robert Redford, smells like Boy George, and dances like Michael Jackson.

Claude's strictly a goin' out man who wouldn't stay home on Friday and Saturday night if he knew Sally was on the way over (skin-tight jeans an' all) with a five-gallon bucket full of daiquiri's, a case of longneck Bud, three Alabama tapes, and divorce papers three days old.

"Might miss somethin'," Claude would say.

Miss somethin'?

What, pray tell? What, Claude?

THE HEART BREAKER

I was over at Mel's Juke and Bobby-Q when I saw ole Rooster tryin' to move in on the gal over by the juke box.

"Hey, Rita!" he yelled at Robbie Nell's partner.

"Yeah, whatcha' want, Rooster, a beer?"

"Naw, give that ol' gal over there by the juke one an' tell her I bought it," he ordered. Then, turning back to me he said, "Set y'sef down if y'want to."

I pulled up a chair, propped my foot in it and watched Rita deliver the beer and the message to "that ol' gal" who, by my arithmetic, measured in the neighborhood of 37–22–36, and that ain't a bad neighborhood. Once, when she stood to adjust whatever women stand up to adjust, I had to change my calculations because if those jeans with the little pony on the back pocket ever busted, the measurements would change to 37–22 and a bunch. Swift never packed a tighter package.

Rooster sent a steady stream of Blue Ribbons to "that ol' gal" and finally made his move shortly after midnight when he called Rita, peeled a ten-spot off a roll, and said, "Tell them jokers to play my song." Rita was well-schooled and shortly them jokers played "For the Good Times," and Rooster danced with "that ol' gal." The jeans held, thank God.

When the song ended, Rooster returned to his table and propped.

"You really like that song, huh? I asked.

"Only one I dance to, Hoss. You can have that fast mess. I ain't dancin' with no gal I can't squeeze."

Country songs are mostly sad songs with such tear-jerking lines as "Three hungry children and a crop in

136

the field; You picked a fine time to leave me, Lucille," "Ruby, don't take your love to town," "When your girlfriend writes a letter to your wife." Sad words, sure, but not nearly as sad as those sung to Rooster by "that ol' gal."

She was busy collecting her Salem 100s and Bic lighter and stuffing her shoulder bag when Rooster hit her with, "Come on, baby. Let's go to my place down on the river."

"Can't. Goin' to S'vanner with the guitar picker," she said. The saddest lyrics ever written? You better believe it. After Rooster invested twelve dollars in beer and the guitar picker hadn't even bought her a Slim Jim, she comes up with, "I'm goin' with the guitar picker."

Rooster watched him put his Fender electric in the case, grab what was left of the last Blue Ribbon Rita had delivered to "that ol' gal," and leave with her. Rooster couldn't believe it.

"Damn, Rita! He looks like a commercial for embalming fluid. What's he got that I ain't got?" Rooster asked.

"I can tell you but you won't like it, Rooster."

"Go ahead!"

"A Fender electric guitar that he knows how to pick, 'that ol' gal' you been buyin' beer for all night, and what's left of the last Blue Ribbon you bought her."

"Yeah, guess you're right. I'll wait for you in the truck, Rita."

"Ten-four, Rooster."

I left and headed home, thinking about Rooster. Somebody ought to write a song about him. I hummed the lyrics, sad lyrics, as I tooled up U.S. 1 on my Harley: "Sorry, but I'm goin' with the guitar picker."

DON'T MESS WITH THIS REDNECK'S MAN

I guess it must have been about 10 P.M. when I next heard it. I was standing in the Golden Corral parking lot talking to a friend when a woman behind us muttered in a hushed tone. "There's a big female star in town and I just heard she's gonna' show up at the Ball and Bash at the Elk's Club tonight."

I turned to see who might be divulging such classified information. Barbara Walters? Phyllis George? Tina Hicks? No.

"Who is it?" I asked.

"Don't know her name. Just a big star, that's all I heard," she said.

"Do you think it might just be a rumor?" I asked. "Is your information from a good source?"

"The best. Margie told Mildred who told Christine who told Jane who told Grace who told Mary who told Ann who told me . . . all VERY confidential. So don't breathe it to a living soul," she said.

"Oh, I won't! Not living or dead. I promise." I told her, and headed straight for the Elk's Club.

A STAR IS BORN

I saw the crowd and sensed I had hit paydirt as soon as I walked into the bar. There must have been a hundred fans crowded around the beautiful "star" just hoping to be granted the privilege of touching the hem of her garment.

All I could see was her blonde hair. I immediately climbed in a chair for a better look at the "star." I recognized her right away: Robbie Nell Bell, from Alma, better known in these parts as "Robbie Nail Bail, fum Almer." She was decked out in her best Ball and Bash finery: a red cowboy shirt, jeans as tight as an overwound

138

pocket watch, her ever present Salem Light 100s in her shirt pocket, a Blue Ribbon in her left hand, and a switchblade with a nine-inch blade in her right. And I heard her say in her never-to-be mistaken Almer brogue, "I tol' ya' not to mess with my man! Buster don't daintz no slow daintzes when I'm on the scene sugar. Now then, buzz off!"

I finally got to her after the crowd dispersed. She was hopping mad.

"Robbie Nell, what in the world are you doing here?" I asked, easing the knife from her hand while she held firm to the Blue Ribbon.

"Whadda' ya' say, newspaper man? Oh, me'n Buster just come f'r the party," she said. "Buster's been barred from Mel's Juke down close to Broxton so we went party huntin' an' found this'n."

"Buster? Barred from Mel's? Why, Robbie Nell?"

"Broke a salesman's jaw with a brickbat two weeks ago after Buster had done

warned him twice't," she said.

"Warned him? About what?" I asked.

"Not to daintz so close and keep his hands up," she said.

"Keep his hands up?"

"Right. No strokin' below the waist. Buster jus' plain don't lak that," she said. "An' I don't lak no woman crawlin' all over my man on no daintz floor. If it had a happened in Mel's, I'd a cut 'er, y'can bet y'r typewriter on that."

"What are you doing in Georgia, anyway? I thought you had hit it big as a song-writer in Nashville," I said.

"Jus' down here f'r a few weeks to do some serious partyin' an' promote my new song," she giggled.

"New song? What's the name of it?"

"Never Say 'No' To A 'Yes' Man."

"Did you write it?"

"Ya' better bleeve it! Shoot, I got more hits than the Mafia."

SECTION SEVEN

REDNECK IS AS REDNECK DOES

THE DIFFERENCE BETWEEN A REDNECK AND A GOOD OLE BOY

A redneck will stand in the door at the pool room and announce in a loud voice to one and all, "Well, it's 11:30. Time to go to the house an' eat dinner. An' I'll tell you this, too. If'n my ol' lady's got it ready, I ain't gonna' eat a damn thing; an' if'n she ain't, I'm gonna' raise hell."

A good ole boy will leave the pool room quietly, go home, and help his wife set the table and pour the tea.

A redneck will stand in front of the local Amoco station, chew his Levi Garrett, and repeatedly spit on the sidewalk.

A good ole boy will use a paper cup or step to the side of the building to unload.

A redneck walks around with a chip on his shoulder, constantly looking for an argument or a fight.

A good ole boy will do his best to avoid both, content to roll with the flow. But if pushed into a corner he will whip the daylights out of the redneck.

A redneck will ride around in his pickup, drinking beer, and throwing the empty cans out the window.

A good ole boy will throw his empty cans in the back of the pickup and drop them in a dumpster later.

A redneck spends Sunday mornings changing the oil in his pickup, drinking beer, and fishing.

A good ole boy usually can be found in church with his wife and younguns. He'll change his oil, drink his beer and go fishing Sunday afternoon.

A redneck will roll up his sleeves to his shoulders in order to display his tattos and muscles.

Although he may have both, a good ole boy is content to leave his sleeves down and buttoned.

THE DO'S AND DON'TS OF REDNECKIN'

It should be fully understood by pretenders to the world of redneckin' that redneckin' ain't no fad, no passing fancy or a part-time thing. No, sir! Redneckin' is a way of life, either inherited or acquired.

Certain things brand one a Redneck as surely as a forearm tattoo. Therefore, this section is intended to enlighten the uninitiated and never exposed—Yankees—to the wonderful world of redneckin'. The joy of it awaits those willing to do their homework.

Now then, here are some (but by no means all) of the "Do's and Don'ts of Redneckin'":

Do

● Say "Yes, m'am" and "No, m'am" and "Yes, sir" and "No, sir" to your mama and daddy.

● Get up before daylight even if you have nowhere to go or nothing to do.

● Always carry a pocket knife. Sharpen it periodically on the sole of your shoe.

● Give all your children nicknames.

● Hang out at gas stations and pool rooms a lot.

● Spend at least two hours a day playing video games.

● Eat lots of boiled peanuts.

● Learn to peel and eat (chew) sugar cane.

● Mash your blackheads in public.

● Get a dog, any dog. Teach him to follow you wherever you go, and to wait for you outside gas stations and pool rooms.

● Call all females, except your mama, "gals."

● Read all the literature you can get your hands on about Robert E. Lee. Hang his picture in your living room.

● Learn to tell the difference right off between a possum and a coon.

● Keep your pickup radio

143

tuned to a country music station.

• Pour your coffee in your saucer and leave the spoon in your iced tea glass.

• Practice the art of crushing beer cans with one hand.

• Pay your child support on time.

• Get a motorcycle from somewhere, preferably a Harley Davidson. Park it in front of a juke joint at least once a week. Sit on it and clean your fingernails with a knife. Spit a lot.

• Hang a pair of fuzzy dice and/or a fish stringer from the rear view mirror of your pickup.

• ALWAYS stand when "Dixie" is played. And let out a rebel yell, "Yaaaaaaaahhhaaaaaaaaooooooeeeee!!" when it is finished.

• Wear long-sleeve shirts, and roll the sleeves up as far as you can—even in winter.

• Cash your paycheck at the nearest 7–11 store.

• Get in the habit of saying things like, "Ya' better bleeve it," "Ya' got that right," and "I ain't lyin', Hoss."

• Go to lots of high school basketball games, and cuss' the referees out repeatedly.

• Learn to back an 18-wheeler. And don't forget to kick the tires once in a while.

• Go fishing at least once a week.

• Never work on the opening day of deer or dove season.

• Make regular trips to the wrestling matches, and yell out some of the same things there that you yell out at high school basketball games.

• Try and make an annual trip to Nashville. Spend some time while there on Broadway between Second and Fifth Avenues. Have three or four beers at Tootsie's Orchid Lounge and buy a western outfit or two at The Tony Alamo of Nashville. That will give you instant credibility anywhere in the south. Go to Opryland.

• If you happen to be in South Carolina, buy a big supply of fireworks and smuggle them back home. The young'uns will love it on the Fourth of July and during Christmas. Incidentally, so will the local police.

• Get a bumper sticker that says, "I Seen Rock City."

• Learn to sop syrup.

• Practice until you can make your eggs, grits, ham and biscuits come out even.

• Always eat your steak well done and your eggs fried hard.

• Display a large Confederate Flag prominently either inside or outside your house, or both.

• Have some knowledge of Herman Talmadge, George Wallace, Lester Maddox and J. B. Stoner.

• Applaud at parades when the United States and Confederate Flags pass. The degree of applause for each is strictly up to you.

• In summer, just peel off your clothes and jump in a river or creek.

• If there is a choice to be made between cutting the grass and going fishing, stand up for your rights as a redneck. And if you catch any, invite your friends to your house for a fish fry. And tell your "old lady" to make up some hushpuppies if she gets through cutting the grass in time.

Don't

• Wear sunglasses inside during the daytime.

• Have nothing whatsoever to do with nobody wearing an earring.

• Wear your wrist watch with the face of the watch on the inside of your wrist.

• Wear a pinkie ring.

• Wear your belt with the buckle pointed toward first or third base. Aim it straight for the pitcher's mound.

• Keep your wallet in your front pants pocket.

• Read your horoscope or "Dear Abby." The sports page is where it's at, Hoss.

• Drink hot tea or iced coffee. These are unpardonable sins.

• Watch "The Donahue

Show."

- Remove your hat when eatin' with some ol' gal.
- Order potatoes instead of grits. This is just as bad as drinking hot tea or iced coffee.
- Wear anything chartreuse or lavender.
- Get too close to any man who comes from anywhere north of Nashville.
- Button your top shirt button.
- Even own a tie.
- Forget your mama or daddy's birthday.
- Ever talk about how nice anything is in New Jersey or New York.
- Have nothin' to do with any sports car.
- Eat no meat that ain't fried.
- Eat in no cafe that serves foreign food.
- Leave home to go on any trip of more than 25 miles without a six-pack. And don't head home without another.
- Ever be seen at or near a rock concert.
- Loan your knife, gun or wife to nobody.
- Let nobody from nowhere make fun of the way you talk.
- Read 'less you feel like it. An' if'n ya' do, read Southern: Lewis Grizzard, Ludlow Porch, Paul Hemphill, Robert Steed, Furman Bisher, Jerry Thompson, and Ferrol Sams.
- Go to no concerts 'less the performers play and sing country.
- Buy nothin' made outside the U.S. of A.
- Ever pass up an opportunity to praise the South and run down the North.
- Buy nothin' but white bread. Remember, a redneck wouldn't be caught dead eatin' th' likes of rye or pumpernickle. Plus English muffins and hard rolls are bad news.

THE INVISIBLE SOCIETY: CLOSET REDNECKS

It's true that you can't always tell a book by its cover. Likewise, you can't always tell a redneck by the clothes he wears. And where he lives, the kind of car he drives, what his chosen profession is, or what his educational level might be provide no clues either.

In other words, what you see ain't always what you get.

I'm talkin' 'bout a special breed here, Hoss: closet rednecks. I'm talkin' 'bout the fella' who's all spit an' polish, Mr. Clean during the daytime; but as soon as night falls, his colors change quicker than a chameleon. I'm talkin' 'bout the fella' who has quiche and white wine at the club for lunch and pickled pig's feet and beer at Shorty's Bar and Grill for supper.

I'm talkin' 'bout the fella' who sucks on breath mints in the office all day and pops a wad of Levi Garrett in his mouth the minute he gets home.

I'm talkin' 'bout the fella' who wears three-piece suits, oxford cloth button-down shirts, and Gucci loafers from nine to five and changes into his Levi jeans, Wrangler shirt, Tony Llama cowboy boots, and Stetson cowboy hat before headin' on down to Shorty's.

I'm talkin' 'bout the fella' who walks the straight and narrow all day and turns into a card-carrying, bona-fide, pop-top, put-another-quarter-in the jukebox, so's yo' mama, Rebel-yellin' redneck at sundown.

Closet rednecks, that's what I'm talkin', and they are out there in droves. They're in juke joints and pool rooms from Florida to North Carolina, Georgia to Texas—and all points in between. They're doin' their thing. It's called redneckin',

Hoss. And they belong to the secret society of Closet Rednecks.

I've been around juke joints all my life, and down through the years I've come to know quite a few of the closet redneck breed. In some, the trait is born and bred in them. Others acquire it through association and the desire for a partially different lifestyle, a relaxing, devil-may-care, throw-caution-to-the-wind lifestyle. No matter how they acquire the trait, closet rednecks do their thing.

Social and economic standing has no bearing whatsoever when it comes to closet rednecks. I know one in Louisiana who could buy Texas. By day, he clips coupons and watches the stock market. By night, he hits the redneck bars. Drinks beer and tomato juice.

I know another, a lawyer in Savannah, who's big in real estate. He's a closet redneck, heavy into country music. He'll drive for miles to hear a good country band. The man has more country albums than RCA. He plunks at the guitar for his own amusement and would no doubt give six condominiums if he could play like Chet Atkins.

An excellent example of a true closet redneck is my friend, Jasper D. He was born in Detroit, went to college in Michigan, and became a lawyer. He's a good one, and very successful. Jasper D. met and married a fine Georgia girl and moved south, setting up a law practice in Atlanta. The marriage lasted eight years before the divorce became final. That was five years ago. He hasn't re-married. His law practice is flourishing, and he lives in a fine townhouse in an affluent suburb.

Three years ago, the redneck bug bit Jasper, and today he is no longer Jasper. "Just call me J.D.," he tells his friends. The bug bit hard.

Before the redneck bug bit, Jasper was pretty much the prototype of a big city lawyer. You know, drive to the office in the morning, back home at night. Dinner, a little television, maybe a book. That was it. Not any more.

Jasper ("J.D.") hits the juke joints, drinks beer, knows all the songs on the jukebox at Junior's by number, and shoots pool until midnight. While his favorite restaurant before the bug bit was a fancy Atlanta restaurant, Jasper ("J.D.") can now be found most nights at supper-time at Big John's Barbeque in South Atlanta. It's easy to tell if he's inside; just look for his Honda Goldwing in the parking lot. It'll be the one with the Confederate flag on the windshield.

A few years back I was in a juke joint in South Georgia. The place, Kitty's Korner, was filled with rednecks, male and female. The jukebox was going full blast, pop-tops were popping, the pool table was busy and the television news reporter was receiving no attention. Kitty's was a beehive of activity.

I hadn't been there long when I spotted Earl, an x-ray technician. He was seated at the end of the bar with a cold beer in front of him. His eye caught mine, and he motioned for me to join him, which I did.

"What in the world are you doing here?" I asked. "This is the last place in the world I'd expect to find you."

"Come here all the time," he said, turning up his beer.

"But you ain't no redneck, Earl, and this ain't nothin' but a redneck joint."

"Redneck? What's a redneck? All I know is that these folks in here are my kinda' folks. And the beer's cold," he said. "They work hard, they play hard, and they drink hard. An' they don't ask a man no questions. They don't give a damn who you are or where you come from. Ever'body's equal when they walk through that front door, an' that's a hell of a lot more'n I can say for some places. Buy ya' a beer?"

"Uh, yeah, thanks, Earl."

I drank the beer and left Earl talkin' to the bartender, and some girl. She was barefooted, if that means anything.

Closet rednecks. A man is likely to run into 'em most anywhere.

I have the feeling that sooner or later the real rednecks, the ones who work at it full time, are going to reach the point where they question closet rednecks invading their territory. I wouldn't be at all surprised if they didn't come up with some sort of entrance exam that a closet redneck had to take before he would be allowed to enter the real redneck world, even on a part-time basis. In view of this, I have devised such an exam that the rednecks might consider. Just 10 questions:

1. Have you ever swallowed lard?

2. Do you now, or have you ever owned a motorcycle?

3. Can you bench press a VW?

4. Do you bathe more than twice a week?

5. How many pairs of boots do you own?

6. Which do you carry, a knife or a pistol?

7. Do you know Willie Nelson's middle name?

8. Have you ever totaled a pickup?

9. How many times you been arrested for fightin'?

10. Can you read and rite? How good?

One prime example of a closet redneck is the case of a Birmingham, Alabama, doctor. His wife, Sarah Jane, related to me just how the transformation from M.D. by day to redneck by night takes place.

"You wouldn't believe he's the same man," Sarah Jane says. "All day long he's in his well-appointed and fashionable office seeing patients as the highly respectable medical specialist that he is. He's decked out in his starched-just-right blue button-down oxford shirt, his ultra-conservative tie, banker's gray trousers and black Florsheim tassel loafers. His styled hair is perfectly groomed and he wears just enough Polo cologne to be interesting. His white medical coat is starched to perfection, and his stethoscope is ever-present in his pocket or dangling around his neck. The nine-to-five picture is that of professionalism personified. And his immaculately manicured nails grip the steering wheel of his equally immaculately manicured Mercedes when he drives back and forth to the hospital to see patients and perform surgery."

But, according to Sarah Jane, the good doctor comes out of the closet the minute he arrives at their suburban mansion home from his office. "You wouldn't know he was the same man," she says.

So. What happens to the good doctor when the sun goes down? This is what his wife says:

"The first thing he does is shed his working clothes. Off comes the shirt, tie, conservative trousers and spit-shined shoes. Within minutes, he emerges from the bedroom decked out in his old and faded jeans, cowboy boots, denim shirt, a

Charlie Daniels hat and chewing Levi Garrett tobacco. He heads straight for the back yard and walks right on by the Mercedes like it wasn't there and jumps into his prized vehicle, a 1968 Chevy pickup with oversize tires. He then inserts a Willie Nelson tape and blasts off in a cloud of dust. Where does he go? He just rides and rides, chewing tobacco, spitting and listening to Willie Nelson. Most of the time he's gone for over an hour, and he's happy as a lark when he returns and brakes to a stop behind the Mercedes. What he's done is make the transformation— from surgeon to redneck."

According to Sarah Jane, the good doctor's transformation doesn't end when he parks his pickup. There's more to come after dinner (supper).

"Most nights he retires to the den after dinner for about an hour. He gets on the telephone and calls old friends back home, in Arkansas. And I'll tell you, you would never know it was the same man that spent the day engaged in his profession as

a doctor. The minute he gets on that telephone to Arkansas his entire manner of talking and conversing changes completely. 'How are you?' suddenly become 'How y'all doin'?' and 'How are your parents getting along?' changes to 'How's y'r mommernem?' Such things as 'Shoot I reckon!' 'Ya' better bleeve it! and 'I ain't never', emanate from the den. And when he's finished, does he say, 'Well, you'll have to excuse me, Roger, but I really must go?' Not on your life. It's 'See ya' 'round, Hoss. I gotta' bring this to a screechin' halt.' So you see, I really have two husbands—a surgeon by day and a redneck by night."

After hearing Sarah Jane's story, I am more convinced than ever that there is a definite need for a Closet Redneck Society, a club if you will, that would welcome such men with open arms; a club that would afford such professionals the opportunity to vent their true feelings after a long, hard day at the office. Indeed, a place where they can "let it all hang out."

JUST WHAT IS A REAL SOUTHERNER ANYWAY?

I've always been real proud of my southern heritage. "I'm American by birth and a Southerner by the grace of God" is how the bumper sticker puts it.

My Southern loyalty even extends to my bedroom as I sleep nightly under a 4' × 6' Confederate flag that hangs from the ceiling. Somehow, I feel more secure with that flag above my head.

I love the South for many reasons: the friendliness of its people, the wide open spaces, the diversity of its terrain, the beauty of its women and the delicious taste of its food.

Even on the streets our folks are friendly. Like when you meet a Southerner driving a motor vehicle he raises a forefinger to greet and recognize you. Of course, the folks in New Jersey do the same thing. Only they use a different finger.

As much as anything else, I love Southerners for their ability to poke fun at themselves. And that brings me to the following:

ARE YOU FROM DIXIE? REALLY?

• A real Southerner can sing all the verses of "Amazing Grace" with every book closed and every eye closed.

• A real Southerner thinks every airplane flight in the world passes through Atlanta.

• A real Southern woman knows her place: on the 50-yard line on Saturday afternoons.

• A real Southerner considers himself bilingual if he can understand Yankees when they talk, but will fight you 'til sundown if you call him a bilingual.

• A real Southern church-goer won't speak to other real Southern church-goers in the liquor store.

- A real Southerner puts Tabasco sauce on his hot sauce.
- A real Southern Republican probably moved here.
- A real Southerner is more scared of filter-tipped cigarettes than cancer.
- A real Southerner eats dinner at noontime and supper at night.
- A real Southerner thinks radar was meant for the Air Force and observes the 55-mile an hour speed limit only in his driveway.
- A real Southerner can kiss his girlfriend goodnight without shifting his toothpick or match stick.
- A real Southerner knows that tomatoes aren't any good unless they're grown in the same dirt he walks on.
- A real Southerner would rather have a cold biscuit than a hot tamale.
- A real Southern churchgoer knows whose eyes are not closed during the prayer.
- A real Southerner knows that streak-o-lean is the best part of the hog.
- A real Southern housewife thinks we should have a national holiday for freezing corn and planting bulbs.
- A real Southern husband can't tell you the date of his wedding anniversary, but knows when it's the first day of deer season.
- A real Southerner says, if God hadn't intended us to eat grits then why did He give us red-eye gravy.
- A real Southerner knows that the real purpose of the Mason-Dixon Line is to separate "Y'all" from "You'se Guys."

BUMPER STICKERS WILL TELL YOU A LOT

Has America gone bumper sticker crazy? If so, the South is leading the pack.

Some of my favorites include:

"If You Can Read This—Thank a Teacher. If You Can't—Find One."

"The Rat Race Is Over—The Rats Won."

"Crime Doesn't Pay—Neither Does Farming."

"If Dolly Parton Had Farmed Last Year—She'd Be Flat Busted Today."

"If You Drink, Don't Drive—You Might Run Over A Pothole And Spill Some."

"People With VD Need To Be Shot."

"Dress Designers Know All The Angles."

And this one observed on a runner's car next to a Leprechaun Marathon bumper sticker: "O.K.—Your Pace or Mine?"

Here's one on an enterprising tavern owner's car: "If You Drive Your Husband To Drink—Drive Him To My Place, The R & R Bar, 1250 E. Madison Street."

I get a bang out of bumper stickers. I even have a pair on my medieval Mercury, Maude.

"Thank You For Not Laughing At This Car" and "My Other Car Is A Rolls Royce." but I need one more that reads, "Intensive Car Unit."

I'm thinking of cashing in on the bumper sticker market as soon as my next royalty check clears the bank. Every vehicle from a Toyota to a bulldozer has them plastered on. You can't run a political campaign anymore, have a raft race, promote rock music, or be a born-again Christian without a bumper sticker.

And there are a lot of bumper stickers that haven't been manufactured yet.

Many segments of our society have been seriously neglected and I'd like to correct the situation by opening my own bumper sticker factory.

First off, I need a line of sample stickers. I've taken care of that. Here are just a few that I feel might make the charts:

• "Dieting Is The Triumph Of Mind Over Platter."

• "Fools Rush In—And Grab All The Good Seats."

• "If Everything's Going Against You—You're Probably In The Wrong Lane."

• "If You Think I'm Ugly—You Should See My Twin Sister."

• "Be Reasonable—Do It My Way."

• "Use Our Easy Credit Plan—100 Percent Down—No Payments."

• "I'm a Pacifist—And I'll Kill Anybody Who Says I'm Not."

• "Love Thy Neighbor—But Don't Let It Get Around."

• "Visit Honest Carr—The Used John Dealer."

• "There's An Advantage To Being Poor—The Doctor Will Cure You Faster."

• "A Woman's Work Is

Never Done."
- "A Friend In Need—Is A Pest."
- "The Pope's Files Are Marked 'Sacred' and 'Top Sacred.'"
- "I Got Rich Betting On The Democrats—Now I'm A Republican."
- "Your Man Got Everything? Give Him A Valuable Miniature—Rhode Island."
- "The IRS Believes In Equality—They Love To See Everybody Suffer."
- "Why Does Christmas Always Come When The Stores Are Most Crowded?"
- "If You Knew Susie Like I Know Susie—You'd Go Out With Margie."
- "I Love Everybody— And You're Next!"

In this day of specialization I can't overlook the specialty bumper sticker bonanza. Like these, for example:
For the weight watchers:

- "A Word To The Wide Is Sufficient."
- "Rear Today—Gone Tomorrow."
- "I Can Resist Everything—Except Food and Temptation."
- "Sign Up For Dr. Flabby's 21-Day Diet—And Lose Three Weeks."
- "Miracle Diet: Eat All You Want—Chew—But Don't Swallow."
- "Exercise—The Best Way To Lose Weight. Shake Your Head Back and Forth 'NO!'"
- "Diets Are Strictly For Those Who Are Thick And Tired Of It."
- "If You Are Thin, Don't Eat Fast. If You Are Fat, Don't Eat—Fast."

So what if my bumper sticker business doesn't make it? I'll just make this final one for myself and move on to something else.
- "If At First You Don't Succeed—To Hell With It!"

A REDNECK AND HIS MONEY ARE NOT EASILY PARTED

My friend Robbie Nell Bell and I were talking the other day about how there always seems to be so much month left at the end of our money.

"Bo," she said, "I've figured out a surefire way of keeping out of trouble with my creditors."

She gave me permission to include them in this handbook. "Hell, Bo," she said, "I know at least three people who use them. Works every time!"

So here they are.

• Mail a check for the full amount—but don't sign it. This should get you at least three extra days.

• Place a properly prepared check in an envelope and drop it in the box at the Post Office—but don't put a stamp on it. Many companies refuse to accept "postage due" mail.

• If you happen to be mailing a remittance to a company in Omaha, Nebraska, Zip Code 68101, just substitute the Zip Code 13207 and let the folks in the Syracuse, New York, Post Office worry about it. That should give you about a week.

• If the bill is for . . . oh, say, $132.45 . . . make your check out for $13.24 and send it along. When you hear from your creditor, and you will, send another check along with this valid (?) explanation: "I'm so sorry. I obviously misread the amount due."

• Also, it doesn't hurt to put a picky company on the defensive now and then. Like when they send a third notice threatening legal action. Drop them a note to this effect: "I was surprised to hear from you and learn that I have an outstanding balance. I have been anxiously awaiting the refund

157

that you notified me would be forthcoming last November. Thank you so much." (That should get you ten extra days.)

• Here's an innovative one: "Thank you for your recent correspondence regarding my account. Now that I have your address again I will gladly remit within one week. You see, there was a small fire in my office and while no great amount of damage was sustained, my 'payments due' file was destroyed completely."

• "Thank you for your patience. I should be able to remit after the next term of court which is scheduled for May when my pending divorce trial will be held. However, at present, all my assets are tied up in a joint account with the plaintiff."

• This one has worked well for short delays in the past: "My checkbook was stolen while I was in Atlanta last month and the bank has stopped payment on all checks on my account until the next full moon, which is due the latter part of April."

• "My husband has asked me to notify you that he is progressing well and hopes to be back in his office on a part-time basis within thirty days. The cast is scheduled to be removed on Friday and the stitches will be removed on Monday, provided the infection has cleared up."

• But this one hasn't worked as well as I had hoped for: "All my assets are in the hands of my attorney, Leon Green. While I am not too familiar with the proceeding, he makes repeated references to something called 'Chapter 11,' whatever that is. Have a nice day."

When it comes to paying bills, my favorite character has to be Lem Barton who lives on the outskirts of Willacoochee and raises goats and red wigglers. He developed a novel way of paying his bills.

On the fifth of each month, Lem takes all his bills and puts them in his hat. One by one he draws them out and writes a check for the indicated amount. When his bank balance approaches zero in his checkbook, he stops paying and mails the checks he's written.

The story goes that one month he received a telephone call from an irate creditor who literally raked him over the coals for non-payment. Lem patiently reviewed his hat method of payment to the creditor to no avail. The creditor ranted on and on until finally Lem had heard enough, and told him:

"Well, you just listen to me young feller! If you can't change your tune and be a little nicer, I won't even put your name in the dad-gummed hat next month!"

Bo Whaley has won twenty-one awards as a columnist for the Dublin, Georgia, Courier Herald. He speaks to more than 200 audiences each year, hosts a morning radio talk show, is the author of *Rednecks and Other Bonafide Americans*, "and loafs a lot."